AWN

DATE DUE

THE
SUMMONS
OF LOVE

THE

SUMMONS

OF LOVE

MARI RUTI

Columbia University Press   *New York*

Columbia University Press
Publishers Since 1893
New York   Chichester, West Sussex
Copyright © 2011 Columbia University Press

Library of Congress Cataloging-in-Publication Data
Ruti, Mari.
The summons of love / Mari Ruti
p. cm.
ISBN 978-0-231-15816-9 (cloth : alk. paper) — ISBN 978-0-231-52798-9 (ebook)
1. Love. 2. Responsibility. I. Title.

BF575.L8R8787   2011
177'.7—dc22   2010050833

Columbia University Press books are printed
on permanent and durable acid-free paper.
This book is printed on paper with recycled content.

Printed in the United States of America

c 10 9 8 7 6 5 4 3 2 1

References to Internet Web sites (URLs) were accurate at the time
of writing. Neither the author nor Columbia University Press is responsible for
URLs that may have expired or changed since the manuscript was prepared.

Honey, now if I'm honest, I still don't know what love is.

—David Gray, "The Other Side"

Contents

Contents

Contents

THE
SUMMONS
OF LOVE

Introduction

Romantic love summons us to become more interesting versions of ourselves. It speaks to those dimensions of our being that reach for enchantment—that chafe against the mundane edges of everyday existence. If much of life entails a gradual process of coming to terms with the limitations imposed on us by our mortality (by the tragically fleeting character of human experience), love boldly pursues the immortal. This does not mean that it grants us everlasting life. It cannot, unfortunately, rescue us from the relentless march of the clock. But to the extent that it rebels against the undertow of everything that is trite or prosaic about the world, it touches the transcendent; it ensures that we do not completely lose contact with the loftier layers of life.

Our mortal bodies are always filled with immortal longings in the sense that what we yearn for psychologically and emotionally is often much more ardent than what our human frames can sustain. It is as if our frail bodies were inhabited by the heaving breath of a restless giant. This giant clamors for freedom and recognition. It strives to break the shackles that bind it to the narrow confines of material existence. Yet we have no way of keeping it alive outside of our mortal bodies. The best we can do is to find various ways to feed it within the boundaries of our daily experience; we have no choice but to learn to live with, and even welcome, the excess inner agitation that, time and again, disturbs our plans for calm and unruffled lives.

It would be easy to interpret the fact that our immortal longings do not fit comfortably within our mortal bodies as a curse or a cruel existential joke. Yet the tension between what we are and what we yearn to become is what lends human life much of its innovative energy. Because this tension keeps us from feeling fully satisfied with our lives, it compels us to reinvent ourselves on a regular basis. It repeatedly pushes us into cycles of personal renewal that guarantee that we do not become emotionally stagnant or complacent; it prevents us from becoming bored with ourselves by supplying us with an endless array of new aims, aspirations, and preoccupations. It is, in short, the underpinning of everything that is creative about our lives. And, during our most inspired moments, it connects us to the more sublime frequencies of human experience.

Love as an Existential Nudge

Traditionally, the sublime has been envisioned as what inspires awe while resisting our ability to fully fathom its scope or power. The most common examples of the sublime—stormy oceans, rugged mountains, immeasurable deserts, starry skies, the darkness of night, absolute solitude, or some misfortune of soul-shattering magnitude—possess an enormity, force, or mysterious depth that escapes human control. We can neither tame them nor capture them within the folds of our imagination. Yet the very fact that we feel inadequate in the face of the sublime induces us to stretch our minds so that we can at least draw closer to what eludes us; it invites us to activate a greater range of our conceptual capacities so that we come to fill up more of the space between ourselves and what we cannot attain. This is why the sublime stirs us: it speaks the language of the immortal giant within us.

The same can be said of love. Love ruptures the canvas of our everyday experience so that we feel transported beyond the ordinary parameters of our lives. The French critic Julia Kristeva conveys this perfectly when she states that love gives us the impression "of speaking at last, for the first time, for real." It allows us to feel fully and exuberantly alive, as if we were finally saying something enormously significant. If the normal organization of our lives tends to be a bit monotonous, love represents a sudden fissure—an unexpected break, swerve, or deviation—in that organization. This is why we often experience it as a stunning revelation that allows us to view the world from an unsullied perspective. It is as if everything that is dazzling, radiant, hopeful, and untarnished about the world slid into view from behind the familiar screen of our everyday reality. We feel oddly rejuvenated, connected to the deepest recesses of our being. Our daily routine becomes animated so that even its most humdrum facets seem heavy with potential. In this way, falling in love accelerates our personal process of evolution.

As human beings, we are all engaged in this ongoing process. On the one hand, most of us have a strong sense of what gives consistency to our identities—of what makes us "us"—through the passage of time; we are aware of a kernel of personality that gathers our disparate experiences into a semicoherent perception of self. On the other hand, who we are today is never entirely the same as who we were yesterday. And tomorrow will bring yet another edition of "us" into being. Much of the time we evolve at such a snail's pace that we are unaware of the changes we undergo. However, there are times when we are all of a sudden thrust onto a new path—when some unanticipated event or chance encounter alters the entire direction of our lives. Such episodes can be painful or troublesome, for often we are forced onto an unfamiliar route out of necessity, perhaps because the old one has become so riddled with obstacles that it is no longer passable. In such cases, we may be fearful of the nameless monsters lurking around the bend and, therefore, less than keen to proceed. But existential nudges that seem to come out of nowhere and that alter our lives beyond recognition can also feel miraculous, conjuring up a whole new universe of enticing possibilities. Being struck by Cupid's arrow is among the most coveted of such nudges.

The wager of this book is that when we are summoned by love, we are brought to the threshold of an enormous opportunity. Choosing to cross this threshold sends tremors through the sum total of our existence so that, once we have stepped to the far side, there is no turning back. Regardless of how things work out in the end, our lives have been utterly and irrevocably modified. We cannot go on living as usual but must, instead, devise fresh modalities of making our way through the world. This is because whenever we accept love's invitation, we also extend one: we open the door to another person so that he or she can, metaphorically speaking, set up camp within our interiority. The consequences of this are far more radical than we might at first realize, for there is no way to receive a lover into our private domain without renegotiating the basic outlines of our being.

An Invitation to Self-Actualization

In general, human subjectivity is inherently social in the sense that our identities are always shaped by our interactions with others. Without others, we would in fact never acquire a self to begin with. After all, when we are born into the world, we have no conception of ourselves as distinct persons. We have no psychological capacity to speak of. And we have no means of verbalizing our feelings or observations. We are enclosed within a solipsistic bubble where our only way to communicate with the outside world is through tears, screams, gestures, and facial expressions. It is the presence of others that, over time, rescues us from this state of primordial helplessness.

It is through those who surround us that we learn to speak, develop an intricate inner life, and come to understand our emotions and experiences. Without others, we would never find a way to insert ourselves into the elaborate rhythm of the world; we would never be able to settle into a life that makes (at least some) sense to us.

Over the span of our lifetimes, our personalities solidify through our repeated interactions with others. In other words, our self-image is always dependent on the responses of those around us. However, some of the people we meet have much more influence over our destinies than others. And no one is more powerful than the person we love. Because falling in love by definition entails an opening-up to an other that is much more intimate, much more profound, than our "normal" interpersonal interactions, it can push us to question what we typically take for granted. Particularly when love causes us to lose our footing—when it disorients and bewilders us—it ushers us into an alien landscape that compels us to widen our emotional repertoire. We are asked to adopt a language that we do not entirely comprehend and that we do not speak with any degree of fluency; we are urged to make room within our psyches for what is always slightly unknowable and often thoroughly unpredictable. We are, in short, transported to the periphery of our habitual universe, which means that we have no choice but to expand our inner horizons.

The disorganization that love brings to our lives thus contains the seeds of new ways of approaching our existential undertaking. We are invited to realize inner potentialities that may have hitherto remained largely latent or even completely neglected. This invitation comes to us from the one we love, for when we fall in love, we are often motivated to develop what is most promising about us; we are driven to actualize those parts of ourselves that we sense most merit our attention. What is doubly intriguing about this is that there are usually only a small number of people who have the power to elicit this response from us. Such lovers help us release and foster the spirit—the kernel of personality I referred to above—that is unique to us. In this sense, the lovers we draw into our lives determine, in part at least, the kinds of people we become. Our individual specificity gets molded in relation to those who manage to infiltrate the least frequented corners of our interiority. This is why it is immensely important to choose lovers who enrich us by activating what is generous and life-affirming within us. Indeed, selecting the wrong person can impoverish us to such a degree that we—sometimes for very long stretches—lose our ability to effectively cope with the various challenges of life.

The Risks of Love

Intuitively, we know this. We know that the risks of love are formidable. Yet many of us routinely (and sometimes repeatedly) make dreadful choices. The object of our desire may not return our feelings. Or he or she may turn out to be completely different from what we initially thought; he or she may let us down in countless ways that we cannot prepare for. In other words, the price we pay for love's considerable gifts is that it also renders us unspeakably vulnerable, exposing us to the possibility of the kind of suffering that threatens to crush the very spirit that it helped conjure into existence in the first place. This is one reason that the disappointments of love are particularly bruising, for there is a peculiar brutality to having to resuppress a recently roused (and therefore still fledgling) spirit. There is an intense cruelty to the act of pushing our newly liberated inner giant back into its cage. In extreme cases, doing so puts our very identity at risk by causing an emotional breakdown—a drastic dissolution of being—from which it may take years to recover.

No wonder that many of us find the summons of love anxiety producing. Many of us have backed away from this summons because it seems too volatile, destabilizing, dangerous, or uncontrollable—because it seems to undermine the solidity of our self-understanding. But the cost of declining love's invitation is also high. When we turn away from love because of fear, we refuse to let our inner giant dream of inspiration; we refuse to let it even entertain the possibility of fulfillment. If the disappointments of love may sometimes force us to recage this giant, the alternative of never allowing it to roam free can be even more incapacitating. While a romantic disappointment is usually accompanied by some reward—by some insight we get in return for our pain (provided we are willing to wait long enough)—the complete renunciation of love tends to give us very little in exchange. If anything, it may deanimate our lives so that we over time become more and more accustomed to the idea of settling for the ordinary at the expense of the extraordinary. Sadly, whenever we reach for what is safe and manageable rather than for what awakens the curiosity of our inner giant, we cater to what is commonplace rather than transcendent, with the result that we gradually starve all the curiosity out of our giant.

In this book, I argue that it is important to remain faithful to the summons of love despite its risks. Although it is useful to stay attuned to these risks, and to do everything in our power to avoid making the wrong choices, it is also crucial to come to terms with the idea that love almost by definition requires a high tolerance for insecurity and potential disappointment. This is because it is impossible to decide love's course ahead of time. We cannot determine how things will develop (or cease to develop) in the future. The sense of safety that we often crave in our relationships is always to some extent illusory, calculated to cover over the heart-sinking realization that the minute we allow another person to become precious to us, we must admit that key components of our universe might one day come tumbling down. Since we cannot control how our lover feels about us, we must accept the possibility of losing him or her as part and parcel of every pact of passion we choose to enter into.

Love's Panoramic Calling

We live in a pragmatic culture that tries to convince us otherwise. This culture tells us that there is a way to love without risking ourselves—that love is just like any other aspect of our lives in the sense that we can perfect our performance over time. We are in fact so inundated by practical advice on how to perk up and safety-proof our relationships that it is increasingly difficult for us to remain mindful of the more sublime aspirations of love. We are encouraged to shed the last vestiges of love's mystery by approaching it in the same rational manner as we might approach the task of choosing the right vacation destination or a set of dinner plates. From self-help literature, Internet sites, and magazine columns to talk shows, we are given absurdly levelheaded tips on how to better "manage" our romantic lives so as to minimize the chance of getting burned. We are, in other words, told that there is usually an easy fix to our relationship dilemmas, and that our romantic success is simply a matter of applying this fix before it is too late.

I see *The Summons of Love* as an antidote to this mentality, for it is designed to illustrate that when it comes to romantic relationships, there is no easy fix, and that it is precisely this *lack* of an easy fix that makes love one of the most life-altering forces of human existence. By this I do not mean to say that we cannot improve our relationships, for I believe that there is a great deal we can learn from our past mistakes. But such lessons have next to nothing to do with the cookie-cutter solutions that our society advertises as a way out of our romantic dilemmas. Indeed, I would like to show that love's calling is much more panoramic—much more complicated and comprehensive—than we are, culturally speaking, conditioned to believe. Among other things, we will discover that although love can sometimes make our lives easier and more pleasant, this is rarely its ultimate goal. As a matter of fact, my sense is that there is very little about love that is intended to simplify our lives. Rather, as I have already begun to suggest, its mission is to generate existential turmoil and thoughtfulness so as to prompt us to evolve into more refined, fascinating, and multidimensional creatures. Its main task is to induce growth even when the process required for this growth makes us terrified or uncomfortable.

Because existential growth happens as much through the unexpected obstacles and breakdowns of love as it does through its triumphs, the worst we could do would be to try to turn love into (yet another) logical activity that we can learn to master. Not only are our attempts to domesticate love doomed to fail, but they will extinguish its power to mold our character. In addition, the more we strive to manipulate our love lives, the less authentically we are able to love. Our desperate attempts to control the outcome of our relationships may momentarily alleviate our anxieties about loss and failure, but they cannot in the end secure our happiness. Nor can they ensure the longevity of our relationships. If anything, they make us so cagey and self-conscious that we lose our spontaneous capacity to love. On this view, our efforts to manage love undermine our very ability to experience it. And they also keep us from appreciating the fact that we can usually, over time, find a way to translate even the most devastating of love's blows into personal meaning—that many of life's most poignant and far-reaching insights come to us through the bitter endings and disenchantments of love.

Love as a Gamble

Responding to love's summons means that we must accept a gamble—that we must agree to live out the consequences of our passion regardless of what these might turn out to be. This book is meant to enable us to grasp the full implications of this way of thinking about romance. As opposed to those who assume that love is only worthwhile when it is permanent and harmonious, I propose that heartbreak, dejection, despair, sadness, remorse, and emotional tumultuousness are as integral to romance as are its lighter gradations. Moreover, I argue that without these more shadowy dimensions of love, we might never learn how to adequately respond to the emotional fragility of others; we might never become fully alert to the suffering of those closest to us. Contrary to popular opinion,

I believe that those who have been traumatized by love in the past often make better lovers in the present precisely because they have had a chance to cultivate a more nuanced understanding of love's overall character. As a result, my goal in this book is not only to elucidate the complexities of love, but also to offer consolation to those who have undergone romantic disillusionments.

Although the ideas I develop in this book have been informed by my long-standing academic interest in the fundamentals of human existence—such as how we come to be who we are, how we go about making important life decisions, how we claim agency in the world, how we meet what we cannot control, and what it might mean to lead a rewarding life—it is not a scholarly treatise in the usual sense of the term. Written without footnotes and specialized terminology, it seeks to build a bridge between the intellectual ambitions of the university and the lived realities of the world. Aimed at academics and nonacademics alike, it offers a philosophical meditation on love that is deliberately contemplative rather than prescriptive. The one exception to this open-ended ethos are those moments when I raise ethical questions about interpersonal responsibility and accountability (as I do in chapters 2, 6, and 8, as well as in the conclusion). Such questions demand a degree of critical edge because the ethics of relationality constitutes one of the most charged and confused terrains of both academic theory and popular psychology.

I launch my analysis by outlining some of the most common problems of love. I examine the misguided expectations that we often bring to our relationships, as well as the ways in which we tend to reenact self-destructive patterns of desire. I explain why love frequently functions as a hotbed of unrealistic hopes and ideals. And I clarify why many of us repeatedly fall into configurations of loving that dishearten or demean us. In this context, I demonstrate how we sometimes unwittingly erect obstacles to our own happiness, becoming, as it were, the authors of our own misery. At the same time, I also highlight the exhilarating aspects of romance, particularly the manner in which it empowers us to surpass the customary borders of our identity. I argue that love enables us to resuscitate suppressed facets of our being, allowing us to feel "real" (self-connected) in ways that few other things in life do. In the final chapters of the book, I propose that the losses of love open up avenues of self-development that add depth and substance to our being—that invite us to enter into a process of crafting the kind of character we can be proud of. My hope is that, by the end of the book, it will be clear that even though our loves can be more or less noble, more or less inspiring, the ones that are genuinely transformative are never stale or lackluster. Rather, they discharge a radiance that persists even through our efforts to renounce them. They dislocate (defy and disturb) the boundaries of our everyday consciousness, coating the commonplace with a marvelous kind of luminosity.

[1]

The Hall of Mirrors

It is tempting to see romantic love as an answer to life's difficulties. Many of us have been programmed to believe that love has the power to make us whole, mend our injuries, and give us the meaning of our existence. This is not to say that we are naïve or gullible. Undoubtedly most of us know that seeking our happiness through love is a treacherous affair. We recognize that the act of placing our well-being in the hands of another person can be terribly imprudent. And we understand that looking for a validation of our individuality through the grace and generosity of someone else can get us in trouble. After all, we cannot control how the person in question treats us. There is no guarantee that he or she will make us feel good about ourselves. In addition, when we lose this person's love, we may end up feeling like we have lost a part of ourselves; we may end up feeling like we have lost the core of our identity, so that our lives suddenly seem strangely devoid of worth or direction.

Yet the idea that love holds the key to our salvation—that it possesses the power to complete us in ways that nothing else can—at times beckons us so compellingly that we end up pursuing a romantic alliance at all costs. We may feel that, without love, we will flounder in a limbo of self-definition, incapable of determining how we are supposed to proceed with our lives. We may even come to believe that life without love is intrinsically futile or uninspiring. At its most extreme, our quest for the rewards of love can cause us to neglect other avenues of personal development to the extent that we, over time, become incapable of nurturing the very capacities and characteristics that make us interesting to potential lovers in the first place. We gradually lose the distinctiveness, the alertness of being, that renders us appealing to others. As the French philosopher Simone de Beauvoir observed in the context of warning women against becoming overinvested in love: "One of the loving woman's misfortunes is to find that her very love disfigures her, destroys her."

This may be an overstatement, at least in the contemporary context. Yet there is no question that the overvaluation of love can lead to an impoverishment of character that makes it difficult for us to sustain dynamic relationships in the long run. When we hope that love will banish our impression of being somehow lacking or inadequate, or when we expect from love the kind of unconditional satisfaction that we cannot attain in other realms of life, we may lose ourselves in love's illusory hall of mirrors. When we see love as a shortcut to happiness or fulfillment, we may ignore other means of achieving these goals; we may come to spend our days searching for the special person who is "meant" for us in some cosmic sense. The main goal of this chapter is to illustrate that we are rarely as easily or disastrously mistaken as when we think that we have found the soul mate who completes us.

The Quest for Wholeness

The notion that love leads to an idyllic union of souls has deep roots in Western thought. One of the most celebrated accounts is by the ancient Greek poet Aristophanes, who tells us an evocative story about the origins of love. He explains that a long time ago, in some mythical past, humans had two faces (looking in opposite directions), four arms, and four legs. They were so powerful—so vigorous and formidable—that they aspired to challenge the gods. The gods, understandably enough, became enraged at such a lack of humility. In the end, Zeus decided to punish humans by cutting them in half ("like eggs which are cut with hair") in order to reinstall their sense of modesty.

As a result of this dissection, humans lost much of their strength. They now only had one face, two arms, and two legs. Their confidence vanished with their prowess. Most important, they were filled with a desperate longing to reunite with the half of themselves that they had lost. If the two halves happened to meet, Aristophanes tells us, they threw their arms around each other and embraced in a hopeless effort to grow together again. Their yearning to be merged was so inconsolable that they gradually perished of hunger and complete neglect of all their basic needs. For all his wrath, Zeus did not want humans to die (for this would have left the gods without worshippers). He consequently asked Apollo to move their genitals to the front of their bodies so as to make it possible for them to come together on a temporary (yet recurring) basis. In this way, according to the myth, humans lost their originary sense of wholeness but gained the capacity to reexperience it in fleeting moments of sexual union.

This is essentially a story about the birth of sexual desire. But it is also a fascinating portrayal of the sentiment of wanting to be welded together with another human being that we are taught to associate with "true" love. It gives us a mythological rendering of why it is that we tend to think that love will restore us to a state of self-completion that we imagine we once possessed. It is as if we secretly believed that, like the humans of Aristophanes's story, we have been unfairly robbed of our strength and self-sufficiency and therefore need the compensations of romantic love to reclaim our full humanity. The story clarifies, in a figurative way, why love appears to answer to a yearning in us that we are keenly aware of yet often cannot name or fully express. It explains why love sometimes seems to heal a wound that we were not even entirely conscious of having prior to meeting the person we love.

However, we might as well admit that the idea of an originary wholeness that we have somehow lost in the process of living is exactly what Aristophanes depicts it to be: a myth. In other words, feeling lacking (incomplete and less than perfect) is an important part of what it means to be human. There is no cure for this lack, for the fact is that we never had two faces, four arms, or four legs. There was no wrath of the gods. And there was no primordial dissection at the vengeful hands of Zeus. We were born into this world in a state of vulnerability, and no matter how big a portion of our lives we devote to the attempt to build a personal fortress of safety and certainty, existential security is something that will always in the end elude us.

We might be somewhat consoled if we realized that it is exactly this lack of security that makes us the complex and captivating entities we are—that adds a tragic, poignant, and haunting kind of fragility to human life. Without our vulnerability, we would not be half as interesting as we are. We would, for instance, not be able to approach others with the same degree of empathy or understanding, for our capacity for compassion arises in part from our appreciation of our own acute woundability. Our frailty and existential terror allow us to respond to the frailties and terrors of others. And our moments of weakness make us more tolerant of the weaknesses of those we love. In this sense, our woundability is what lends our characters much of their emotional resonance. It grants us the kind of delicate discernment that enables us to relate to others in caring, thoughtful, and responsible ways. On this view, the attempt to heal ourselves by overcoming our sense of lack might be a largely misguided use of our energies. Such energies might be better spent in learning to value the interpersonal gifts that our brittleness bestows upon us.

Likewise, it might help us to recognize that it is exactly because we feel that we are somehow inherently lacking that we are driven to the kind of inventiveness that characterizes human life at its richest. More specifically, it is precisely because we judge something to be missing from our lives that we feel compelled to conjure up imaginary worlds of possibility. Such worlds, in turn, add vigor and weightiness to human existence on its various levels: the arts, the sciences, institutional structures, politics, religion, and relational arrangements, to name a few. In this sense, the innovative energy that propels human existence—that induces us, over and over again, to reach for the heights of achievement—emerges, in part at least, from our inconsolable awareness of our own deficiency.

One could then argue that much of what we find most worthwhile in the world comes to us from our sense of lack, for it is our repeated attempts to fill this lack that bring into being things of considerable beauty and magnificence. If we felt no lack, we might also not feel any need to compensate for it; we might not feel any urge to create anything new. We might in fact not even have much curiosity about the world and its offerings, for our self-sufficiency would render the world uninteresting. According to this account, it is our lack that not only encourages us to invent imaginary worlds, but also allows us to meet the existing world as a place that might have something of value to offer to us.

Unfortunately, most of us are not used to thinking about our lack as something that vitalizes our existence. Rather, we are prone to experience it as an aching wound in need of mending. And we tend to look to romantic love as our cure and deliverance. In so doing, we sometimes get caught in the web of one of love's most powerful illusions, namely, the idea that another person can conjure away our lack. We in fact place an impossible burden on the person we love, for we ask him or her to grant us the kind of plenitude that is inherently forbidden to us. We ask him or her to accomplish what no one can for the simple reason that human beings are not designed to feel unassailable and entirely self-contained.

It is the very essence of the human condition to never be able to experience the kind of healing union that Aristophanes talks about. This does not mean that romantic love cannot make us feel more self-realized. Or that it cannot alleviate our feelings of alienation. Or that it cannot give us relief from past injuries, grievances, and disappointments. The tender solicitude of a beloved person can go a long way in compensating for the ordeals of life. And certainly, as we will see later, it brings us alive in ways that few other experiences do. However, to the extent that it is our existential assignment as human beings to feel lacking, even love—no matter how loving—cannot make us feel completely whole.

One of the most intriguing implications of Aristophanes's account is that even though Western society holds individuality in high regard, many of us seem to find it quite difficult to bear. On one level, we value the idea of being singular creatures. We may even take pride in our quirks and peculiarities, asserting our right to carve a distinctive path through life. Yet, to the degree that we seek wholeness through those we love, we experience a separation from them as a gaping wound in need of repair. Our fantasies of being able to attain wholeness through a union with others can in fact be so powerful that they come to determine the entire direction of our love lives. At the same time, if we were ever to reach this wholeness, we would lose much of what makes us human—we would lose the raw edge of vulnerability that holds us open to others to begin with. We of course know this. Yet we often cannot help but to yearn for invulnerability.

The Beloved as Mirror

Aristophanes's myth also highlights another, closely related, aspect of love that often misleads us: the fact that our desire tends to be highly narcissistic. In the myth, each lover yearns to be reunited with the lost half of *himself*—the half that was severed due to Zeus's dissection. Although on the surface it may appear that the lover is seeking to fuse with another individual, a deeper look reveals that he is merely aspiring to recover lost facets of his own being. This illustrates what many of us long for in romantic love, namely, the chance to discover dimensions of ourselves in the person we love. All too often we try to turn the other into a flattering mirror that reflects back to us a pleasing image of ourselves. The objective of this kind of love is less to bring two autonomous individuals into a loving alliance than to gratify our longing for narcissistic self-completion. The goal is less to revere the beloved than to fulfill our fantasy of self-actualization.

In real life, the narcissistic undertones of romantic love are usually less overt than in Aristophanes's story. We are rarely literally or consciously seeking a lost half of ourselves. Yet few of us can deny that we are, on some level, hoping that our lover will reinforce our sense of self, and perhaps even make up for some of our deficiencies. We may look for a partner who complements us because he or she possesses characteristics that we do not have. Or we may be attracted to someone who is able to draw out and galvanize disavowed dimensions of our being. This is not necessarily *inherently* problematic. As a matter of fact, later in this book I will argue that a loving encounter between two people can enrich both precisely because it helps each bring to life repressed components of his or her personality. However, love that is primarily narcissistic is more or less fated to deplete both lover and beloved.

One of the most obvious problems with narcissistic love is that it does not respect the specificity of the beloved's being. If the lover's aim, however unconsciously, is to use the beloved as a gratifying mirror, then any aspect of her that obscures the clarity of the image he seeks becomes a nuisance—something to be overlooked, covered over, or pushed aside. The lover, in short, concentrates on certain of the beloved's attributes at the expense of others that might complicate the picture. He is so focused on his own augmentation that only those of the beloved's characteristics that directly prop up his self-regard are acceptable to him. Over time, he builds a one-dimensional image of her that does not reflect her self-understanding. She may feel admired and even raised on a pedestal, but she also senses that she is being deprived of her personhood—of what she, in the intricacy of her being, is or has the promise to become.

While such containment is at times blatant, more often it takes the form of a subtle and indirect (and therefore all the more insidious) denigration that makes the beloved feel oddly censured or disparaged for who she is. This can over time curb her self-expression to such an extent that she comes to feel suffocated within the relationship without knowing why this is the case. She gradually gets the impression that unless she embodies specific traits—unless she fits into the design of her lover's life in precise ways that meet some predetermined (yet often unarticulated) ideal of his—she is worthless in his eyes. She may even attempt to locate the cause of her wretchedness within herself, for she does not necessarily understand that there is absolutely nothing wrong with her particular qualities, but that the problem is, rather, that these qualities do not meet the narcissistic fantasies of her lover. In such instances, there is next to nothing that the beloved can do to fix things, for no matter how she chooses to act, no matter how diligently she tries to improve herself, she will never be good enough for her lover. What he is looking for is an idealized image that coincides seamlessly with his wants and desires. This is something that she can never be.

The Pitfalls of Narcissism

I have here talked about the beloved as a woman because it is women who have traditionally—more often than men—been expected to impersonate the mirror. They have been taught to erase their personalities in order to provide a lucid and uncluttered surface for men's narcissistic fantasies. They have been asked to conceal or downplay the particularities of their being so as to more accurately reflect men's desire. It may in fact be that our culture associates women with mirrors—and with the vanity and narcissistic superficiality that mirrors imply—in part because women have had to stifle the idiosyncratic vitality of their personalities in order to turn themselves into the flat (safe and reassuring) mirror that is demanded of them. As Virginia Woolf once remarked: "Women have served all these centuries as looking-glasses possessing the magic and delicious power of reflecting the figure of man at twice its natural size."

This may account for the stiff formality and self-consciousness of some feminine self-presentations, for the more a woman internalizes the role of a mirror, the less her individuality and characteristic spontaneity remain visible to others. The self as mirror is an artificial self, an empty and well-defended shell that is constructed to please the outside world, but that does not reflect the individual's passions or deep personality. Indeed, such a contrived self is designed to conceal everything that is most eccentric about the woman so that nothing offends, nothing stands out of place or alarms. Like the softly lit mirrors of exclusive hotels and restaurants, such a woman reflects back to her lover an image of himself that he wishes to see: more flawless, more appealing, and considerably more charming than the one he meets in his own bathroom mirror on Monday morning.

In today's society, where traditional gender roles and inequalities have thankfully eroded (even if they are far from being abolished), it might be misleading to analyze narcissism along gendered lines. It may well be that many women are, these days, as guilty of it as men are. Furthermore, narcissism penalizes both lover and beloved, albeit in different ways. If the beloved is drained of her inner complexity, the narcissistic lover also narrows his life-world because he tends to sideline those aspects of his personality that do not correspond to his idealized image of himself. He tends to overlook or actively spurn those of his characteristics that do not comfortably fit within the frame of his mirror. Over time, he becomes a drastically impoverished version of what he could be if only he allowed himself to disobey his own ideal. Although the unconscious goal of narcissistic love is to enhance the lover's self-esteem, its actual result is frequently to fix him into an identity that leaves little room for improvisation.

What is more, such a lover tends to be so dedicated to locating a partner who meets his narcissistic needs that he may get utterly trapped in an unachievable fantasy. He may become attached to an overly specific image of desirability, looking for the kind of woman he will never find for the simple reason that she does not exist in the real world. She is a fantasy that has a viable life only in his mind. A man in this predicament finds that every woman disillusions, disappoints, or falls short in one way or another. Even a woman who initially seems to correspond to his specifications will in the final analysis prove herself undeserving and unremarkable.

Such a pattern of relating keeps the narcissistic lover from embracing the real-life options available to him. He is so focused on attaining his ideal that he forgets to live in the present, shunning the opportunities and possible loves that come his way because they do not live up to the precision of his expectations. Instead of relishing what he could in fact achieve—such as a loving connection that is rewarding without being perfect—he allows himself to be swept into mesmerizing delusions that prevent him from fully entering the stream of his existence. Because such delusions direct his attention to the hazy horizon of what might one day come to pass if only certain conditions were miraculously fulfilled, they hold him at a safe distance from having to actually live his life; they serve as a highly sophisticated defense against the tangible tumult of dwelling in the world. One could even say that they signify a peculiar kind of cowardice, for a person caught up in an unattainable ideal can convince himself that he never has to make a decision or commit to an action.

Making a decision or committing to an action is intrinsically hazardous. One could always be wrong. One's decision or action could have disastrous consequences. Against this backdrop, nothing is more reassuring than ideals that cannot be achieved, that can forever be approached but never actually attained. Such ideals offer a paradoxical kind of protection against existential mistakes because they detach us from the (admittedly byzantine) task of living. But the flip side of this is that they also serve as a convoluted means of reducing the stakes of our existence. When only those encounters or amorous possibilities that resonate with our ideals register on our emotional radar, we miss out on a lot of pleasures that can only arise in the context of a more welcoming relationship to the world—one that embraces the world regardless of how imperfect or deficient it is. In this sense, a life built on ideals is intrinsically limiting—a tepid and tremulous shadow of what it could be.

The Specificity of Desire

Our narcissistic ideals, as well as our yearning to be rescued from our lack, operate on unconscious levels that can lend an astonishing specificity to our desire. We may have all sorts of conscious designs about the kind of lover we should be looking for, the kind of life we should aspire to create, and the kind of relationship we should aim to have. Yet we frequently discard these designs for the sake of some tiny detail that piques our interest in the appearance or demeanor of a complete stranger. We grow enthralled by the tone and timber of a person's voice. We become fascinated by the graceful outline of her lashes, the calm confidence she exudes when put on a spot, her manner of touching her hair, or the way she turns her head to meet our gaze. We are captivated by the shape of someone's collarbone, eyebrows, or fingernails. Or by the way in which the blue of his eyes sparkles in sunlight. The curve of a smile or the warmth of an arm that we accidentally brush against can momentarily become the focus of our entire being. In such cases, our rational understanding of whom we are meant to desire proves perplexingly powerless in the face of some minor characteristic of a person who inexplicably compels our attention.

We meet countless people in our lives. Of these, we like and befriend quite a few. And a small portion stimulate our desire. We may consider those who belong to this portion as romantic possibilities without feeling any particular urgency. We may even have a light-hearted affair with a few of them. But usually there are only a handful of people whom we desire with a burning intensity. Ironically, such people are extremely unlikely to enter our lives through our deliberate efforts. More often than not, they take us by surprise, awakening our desire in ways that are as startling as they are compelling. When this happens, when we all of a sudden feel that only *this* person will do, it is likely that we are being driven by unconscious torrents of narcissistic desire that connect us to the person in question. It is likely that our longing reflects the fact that something about this person corresponds to our most entrenched fantasies of self-completion. The person who fascinates us—who seems to accurately "answer" the requirements of our desire—does so because he or she in one way or another activates our unconscious hunger for wholeness; he or she manages to fill the gaps of our being in ways that we experience as deeply enlivening.

Once we get to know a person, we gain an appreciation for the intricacies of his or her character. But the detail that initially catches our eye and pulls us toward that person is often amazingly trivial, miniscule, superficial, or insignificant. Additionally, we are usually not able to name what it is that triggers our interest. We may be vaguely aware that there is something about a person's "air," "aura," or "bearing" that charms us, but we cannot put our finger on it. We speak of "chemistry" to describe the curious allure that some people hold for us without having any clear idea of what we mean. Attraction, in this sense, is inscrutable and intangible. Part of the enchantment of love—and particularly of its delightful beginnings—arises from this impenetrable element.

The mysterious specificity of desire can add a dash of adventure to our love lives, for we tend to be excited by what we cannot fully understand. And it is not even necessarily the case that this type of desire is always mistaken. As I will illustrate in chapter 7, sometimes it can be an eerily accurate measure of romantic potential. Nevertheless, it is useful to remind ourselves that desire such as this can be profoundly ungenerous in exactly the manner I have described. Inasmuch as it arises from the lover's unconscious fantasy life rather than from any real interest in the beloved's needs, wants, interests, or personality, the beloved is not treasured for who she is. In fact, the minute she exhibits characteristics that do not coincide with the particularities of the lover's desire, or that somehow mar the faultless image that she is expected to reflect back to him, he becomes annoyed or frustrated. His desire is self-interested in the sense that he is unwilling to respect parts of her being that appear superfluous or incomprehensible to him—that grate against the contours of his fantasy world. The moment the beloved ceases to stick to the glamorous persona that the lover wants from her—the moment the singularity of her being asserts itself—he finds his desire waning.

The Speck of Corruption

One of the main limitations of narcissistic desire, then, is that it tends to die a quick death the instant reality intrudes and the engrossing illusion crumbles. As the French theorist Roland Barthes explains, the death of desire begins the moment the lover detects in the beloved a small "speck of corruption"—a minor detail that tarnishes the beloved's revered image. This detail (a gesture, an attitude, a tone of voice, a piece of clothing) is frequently something that unexpectedly renders the beloved banal in the eyes of the lover. Such a detail dilutes the beloved's luster by connecting her to the commonplace routines and platitudes of the world. As a result, she comes to seem embarrassingly ordinary, a source of shame rather than of gratification.

When the magic mirror shatters, the beloved's dazzling image swiftly yields to a paltry and hackneyed reality. Where the beloved once resonated evocatively, the lover now only hears the dreary notes of dull conventionality. Interestingly, the lover does not usually experience his beloved's flawed image as devastating or threatening; he is not personally humiliated in any way. Rather, he grieves the failure of the world to meet his desire. As Barthes specifies, a lover who still believes in his dream aspires to protect the sanctity of his beloved against the corruptions of the world. However, this attitude of devotion falls apart the moment he discerns "on the skin of the relationship, a certain tiny stain, appearing there as the symptom of a certain death."

The death of desire can thus be as mysterious as its inception. We usually do not know why desire awakens. And, similarly, we do not always know why it dies. When we think of the anguish of romantic love, we tend to focus on what it feels like to love a person who does not love us back, or who does not love us in the way that we would like to be loved. We tend to focus on the excess of our desire—on how mortifying it is to want more than to be wanted. Yet, if the intensity of our desire causes us distress, our inability to maintain it over time may be just as agonizing. Indeed, it is difficult to say what is more tragic: not being able to banish unrequited desire or not being able to sustain our desire for a person we love. As wounding as it can be to not have our desire reciprocated, it is equally distressing to not be capable of desire when we would sincerely like to feel it. There can in fact be a terrible sadness to the realization that our desire has waned. In this sense, sometimes the real calamity of love is not the loss of the beloved person through betrayal or abandonment, but rather the loss of the desire that made a connection between self and other possible in the first place.

The appearance of a tiny speck of corruption on the surface of our love is the moment of truth that either makes or breaks our relationship. It is a moment that every relationship will sooner or later face. However, the more our love has been based on illusory fantasies of rescue and redemption—and the more we have elevated our partner to a mirror that caresses our narcissistic self-conception—the more drastic the drop will be. It is not necessarily at all the case that the other has changed. It is just that over time we come to detect aspects of his or her being that we initially overlooked. As I have emphasized, whenever we hope that the other will meet our ideal of perfection, we are likely to ignore dimensions of his or her personality that diverge from this ideal. As a consequence, when the latter intrude, we feel cheated. Sometimes we even accuse the other of having misled us. Yet it was our fixation on our preconceived ideals that made us see only what we wanted to see and fail to notice the rest.

Lovers who manage to sustain a relationship beyond the inevitable moment when a stain or a speck of corruption disturbs the smooth façade of their love are able to love beyond ideals. Their love survives the splintering of the mirror not only because they realize that they will be unlikely to ever find a love that is completely devoid of such stains or specks, but also because they tolerate their mutual humanness. They appreciate, and actively seek to cultivate, the particularity that makes each of them a unique individual. They are willing to sacrifice the pristine flawlessness of their ideals for the messy reality of two people doing their best to relate to each other on the basis of what is inimitable about each. They do not attempt to change each other, or to fit each other into preexisting schemas of perfection. Each of them is able to accept the radical "otherness" of the other—the ways in which the other is nothing like the self—without being either bothered or intimidated by it. Each recognizes that it is precisely this otherness that makes their loved one the intriguing creature he or she is. And each knows that it is only through an honest encounter with this otherness that they—and the relationship itself—can evolve. For such lovers, the integrity of the person they love is more prized than even the most enticing of love's illusions could ever be.

[2]

The Patterns of Passion

Those of us who have loved more than once know that there is often a peculiar kind of consistency to our romantic lives, and particularly to the ways in which we get hurt. There are patterns and emotional scenarios that we tend to repeat over and over again, even when we make a conscious decision to avoid them. We may begin a new relationship confident that we will be able to sidestep familiar traps. And we may be determined to implement new ways of resolving tensions so that, no matter what happens, we will not find ourselves disrespected or trampled on in the same ways as we have been before. We may even choose our partner based on the assessment that he or she will allow us to do things differently. Yet it is often precisely when we believe that we have finally freed ourselves of a pattern or a relational configuration that we once again find ourselves repeating it.

The fact that past patterns return and repeat in the present implies that, whatever our past holds, it animates the present: the present is always infused by the energies of the past. In this sense, there is no such thing as a present that is completely liberated from the past. While this is the case in all aspects of our lives, it is particularly relevant in the context of love. We always bring our entire history of longing to our love affairs. And it is very difficult for us to cope with the realization that the yearnings we carry from the past may not be any more likely to be fulfilled in the present than they were in the past. We hope against hope that our present love can compensate for the devastations of the past. Or that we will finally find a means to redeem the mistakes we have made over the years. It is all the more distressing, then, to face those moments when we realize that the past has managed to catch up with us even though we have done our best to resist its power.

Some of love's repetitions are relatively easy to comprehend. We may, for instance, be more or less deliberately trying to find a substitute for a special love that we have lost. We may be looking to reiterate a past passion that we are having a hard time leaving behind. We may choose a new lover based on the fact that something about him or her reminds us of the person we once loved. We may even be aware that our current lover is merely a pale reflection of our past partner. We may know that we are attempting to reincarnate a lost love whose memory lingers within our emotional landscape. In such cases, repetitions hardly come as a surprise. However, most of the time when the past returns and repeats, we do not understand why. And, most times, we are far from being thrilled at the sudden reappearance of old demons.

The Compulsion to Repeat

It was Sigmund Freud who gave us the tools to understand why our lives—and especially our love lives—exhibit debilitating repetitive patterns. He recognized that our earliest childhood experiences, particularly ones that are somehow traumatic or distressing, leave a permanent imprint in the unconscious recesses of our interiority.

And he argued that the rudimentary outlines of our personality congeal around this imprint so that the patterns of relating that we internalize at this formative period are the ones that keep resurfacing in our lives. No matter how we later choose to conduct ourselves, no matter what kinds of conscious decisions we make, or what kinds of experiences we undergo, these patterns remain engraved within our private universe. Their power is in fact so immense that they determine the basic design of our emotional lives. Regardless of how many layers of complexity we add to our personality in the course of our existence, a trace of this design remains lodged in our psyches.

We start our lives in a state of utter vulnerability in relation to those who care for us. These early relationships of care can be more or less competent, more or less nurturing. Some are characterized by an abundance of love; others are deficient or outright abusive. Either way, the care we receive as infants and young children gives us a blueprint for human relationships, teaching us how to love and be loved. Because the young child's desire for love is invariably larger than what can realistically be provided, infantile experiences are never entirely satisfactory. Indeed, part of what we need to learn at that stage in life is how to cope with the disappointment of not always getting what we want; we need to come to terms with the recognition that our demand for love will not be consistently met. Nonetheless, some forms of care are obviously more conducive to the development of a satisfactory emotional life than others. In this sense, a great deal depends on the cards we are dealt at birth.

Our early experiences of care teach us what to expect from those who love us (or are supposed to love us). We learn the boundaries of acceptable behavior. We develop a sense of the emotional scenarios that we are able or willing to endure. And we find out what kinds of actions are (or are not) effective in interpersonal situations. We, in short, adopt an unconscious set of assumptions that governs the way in which we approach our relationships. Some of us believe that the world is an inherently generous place and that the relationships we form will be loving and sustaining. Others, in contrast, imagine that the world is intrinsically disappointing and that other people are likely to treat us unkindly or even ruthlessly. Those of us who are hugely unfortunate learn that love is always coupled with abuse so that we come to associate it with suffering and do not think twice about it when this is what our relationships deliver.

Our emotional composition is fortunately so elaborate that it would be impossible to draw any direct causal link between our early experiences and the unfolding of our love lives. Nevertheless, if we are not careful, the set of expectations that we bring to the world can have a tremendous impact on the ways in which we interact with others, as well as on the ways in which others respond to us. It is hardly surprising that a person who approaches others with the assumption that she will be treated with respect and compassion will elicit a different response from one who expects—and therefore perhaps also to a certain extent tolerates—ill-treatment.

The fact that our earliest modes of relating leave a lasting trace in our unconscious lives clarifies why we tend to reenact certain emotional scenarios while finding others extremely difficult to achieve. The patterns of passion that we repeat involuntarily, against our will or better judgment, as it were, indicate that we are often motivated by an uncanny faithfulness to unconscious emotional intensities that may have little to do with our conscious inclinations. Freud demonstrated that this unconscious "compulsion to repeat" can be so commanding that we get the impression "of being pursued by a malignant fate or possessed by some 'daemonic' power." In other words, even though the repetitive configurations that burden our existence originate from our own psyches, we experience them as a mysterious hand of destiny that determines how our lives will turn out. We feel that we are in the claws of some impersonal or automatic entity that brings us to the same spot over and again despite our ferocious efforts to arrive at a different destination. Yet it is our own unconscious that keeps spinning the wheel of our fortune.

Repetition as World-Structuring

Most of us are familiar with the idea that the unconscious contains special forms of wisdom and deep insight. We know, for example, that creativity calls for a fluid interchange between our conscious and unconscious lives. For some of us, dreams—which, according to Freud, give us a privileged access to the unconscious—are a significant source of inspiration. Many of us also understand that our unconscious communicates hidden desires that constitute an essential component of our identity. However, Freud's point about the repetition compulsion is that our relationship to our unconscious may sometimes be entirely passive, complacent, mechanical, and uncreative. Whenever this is the case, the unconscious ends up shaping our lives without our conscious consent.

Even the most distressing of our past experiences can be worked with—or, to borrow Freud's terminology, "worked through"—as long as we recall them on the conscious level. In contrast, traumas that remain repressed (kept below the surface of our consciousness) cannot be worked through, with the result that they erupt in unconscious repetitions that cause us, time and again, to relive the pain of the past. We may in fact end up reenacting traumatizing events so consistently that we gradually become more and more firmly trapped in unyielding patterns of relating and self-understanding. And we are particularly liable to do so in the realm of romance for the simple reason that our formative experiences of care—the experiences that gave us our elemental blueprint for loving—take place so early in our lives that they are not reachable through conscious memory. The initial sediments of our emotional lives are so thoroughly buried that they cannot easily be accessed in adult life. From this point of view, we are to a certain extent destined to repeat the mistakes we make in love.

What is especially tragic about such repetitions is that they represent a desperate attempt to right the wrongs of the past. That is, they occur because we are unconsciously trying to "master" a traumatic interpersonal dynamic that has caused us pain in the past. We are driven to a given repetition because, on a fundamental level, we believe that *this* time things will be different, that *this* time we will not get wounded. We are persuaded that repeating an agonizing scenario one more time will allow us to modify its outcome and therefore to transcend those aspects of our history that weigh us down. Unfortunately, as long as we stay within the repetition—as long as we trust that reenactments lead to inner transformation—we will accomplish little, save deepen the injuries we are endeavoring to mend.

Unconscious patterns can be stunningly tenacious and narrow-minded. While our conscious lives show an awareness of personal history, of the ways in which our past, present, and future fall on a continuum that accounts for the overall development of our character, the unconscious preserves archaic passions in an unchanging form. It is characterized by a "timeless" loyalty to antiquated relational designs that can be radically at odds with the demands of our ever-shifting interpersonal contexts. It resurrects past conflicts and ambivalences in a stubbornly frozen fashion, frequently hauling us into modalities of thought and action that are entirely inappropriate to the situation at hand. For example, we may under- or overreact emotionally, aim our love or wrath at individuals who merit neither, or drastically misjudge what really matters in a given scenario. In such cases, our unconscious revives our past within the present in awkward and counterproductive ways.

If we do not find a way of processing our unconscious patterns, they can over time determine what we find imaginable in our lives. As the contemporary psychoanalyst Jonathan Lear puts the matter, unconscious expectations that organize our lives in obstinately repetitive ways are "world-structuring" in that they present a confining set of life possibilities as though they were the only ones we have. Because we treat our customary world as the only plausible world, we have trouble envisioning viable alternatives. We come to expect certain outcomes and, sadly, these are more often than not exactly what we receive. We find ourselves drawn to certain kinds of situations, behaviors, and relationships while viewing others as inherently inconceivable. In this way, what we unconsciously conceive to be the limits of our experience curtails the range of our life options.

Our compulsion to repeat can therefore direct us to hollow and insipid existential paradigms. Because it can make us feel as if our lives were lived by some entity other than ourselves, we can end up becoming the passive spectators of our own experience. Alternatively, the repetition compulsion can set up the conditions of our chronic romantic disappointment. It can, for instance, cause us to ask for love in ways that are destined to fail or backfire. Or it can induce us to select lovers who increase our desolation by treating us in ways that resonate with past experiences of trauma. We may gravitate to uncaring or forbidding lovers while avoiding others who might be able to care for us in more satisfying ways. In this manner, we close off potentially rewarding relational opportunities before they have had a chance to materialize as real-life possibilities.

The reverse of this is that unconscious repetitions can encourage us to have unreasonable expectations for our relationships. They can prompt us to make unrealistic claims on our lovers, so that we end up insisting that they conjure away our past discontents or help us locate the purpose of our existence. Even worse, they can drive us to read others through a simplifying lens that flattens their character, thereby making it difficult for us to approach them in genuinely open-minded ways. Rather than appreciating the distinctive cadence of their spirit, we come to treat them through categories of experience that make sense to us for the simple reason that they are familiar to us from the past. This may ease our discomfort in the face of relational complexity. However, it can also make us extraordinarily intolerant, for we are seldom as ungenerous toward our lovers as when we engage in such unconscious reductions.

Because unconscious repetitions replicate the past in a predictable fashion, they offer us an illusory sense of continuity: they make the future appear foreseeable. The fact that they tend to provide a continuity of sorrow rather than of joy is counterbalanced by our conviction that at least we know what to expect. Over time, repetitions can even make us reconciled to our "fate" in the sense that we begin to imagine that things happen in certain ways because it is our particular lot in life to continue living as we always have. We may even come to view ourselves as being uniquely cursed in relation to specific types of experiences, as if we were condemned to a life of recurring misery. Yet we may also take a secret pleasure in the idea that alternative possibilities remain mere possibilities—that their fulfillment is infinitely postponed. After all, an unrealized possibility by definition persists as a tantalizing potentiality. This, though, in no way alters the fact that our psychological limberness has been compromised; it does not change the fact that we suffer from a strangulation of our emotional lives.

Missing Our Step

None of us are free of psychological trigger points. This is why Freud maintained that there is no such thing as a completely healthy or well-adjusted human psyche: all of us are in one way or another pathological. What varies are the kinds of pathologies we exhibit and how serious or debilitating they are. Given that this is the case, and that all of us are prone to the compulsion to repeat, it is useful to be patient with both our own patterns and those of others. Indeed, it might be a good idea to aim for a kind of solidarity of vulnerability in the sense that we recognize that, all of us, without exception, are likely to miss our step once in a while. It may even be helpful to recognize that our compulsive patterns are an important part of what makes us unique. As painful as they may be, they are also, in a sense, what allows us to feel "at home" with ourselves. In other words, what we most care about on the unconscious level can be as crucial a part of us as are the things that we consciously choose to do; it molds us into the sorts of persons we are.

What makes the repetition compulsion so tricky is that we cannot spot it ahead of time. We cannot predict in the beginning of a new relationship whether or not it is going to activate the compulsion. And we cannot even begin to anticipate the specific manner in which the past might resurface. Even when we cautiously look for signs that our new lover might have certain familiar characteristics, and might therefore end up treating us in ways that we would prefer to avoid, we are unlikely to interpret the situation correctly. An obvious reason for this is that we cannot immediately know another person well enough to make an accurate assessment of his or her character; it takes time for our lover to reveal the details of his or her personality. But an equally powerful reason is that how others behave toward us is always conditioned by our expectations and reactions.

The way we approach our partner may bring out attributes and modes of behavior that are not particularly typical of him. He may be as surprised as we are when he injures us, makes us feel insignificant, or instigates emotional scenarios that we thought we had put to rest a long time ago. There is something profoundly disconcerting—both for us and for our lover—about the moment when archaic childhood feelings flood back with a devastating intensity. By the same token, it can be distressing to recognize that, despite our best efforts to forge a loving dynamic, our present relationship is replicating the humiliation of past alliances. Though it is always possible that we have chosen a malicious partner, or that he possesses a fundamental character flaw that has nothing to do with us, it may also be that there is something about the way we interact with him that is setting off his defenses and hidden aggressions. As a result, he no longer meets us from a place of benevolence, but rather from the most withholding and condescending parts of his being.

I want to be careful here. I do not mean to say that we are to blame for our partner's hurtful behavior, or that our partner should not be held responsible for his or her unkind actions or statements. I am in fact deeply distrustful of contemporary popular psychologies that are premised on the idea that, no matter what others do or say to us, we are solely responsible for our own feelings. These psychologies usually draw a distinction between the actions of others and our interpretation of these actions, alleging that whenever we get hurt or angry, it is because we are interpreting the situation in ways that are painful or infuriating to us. The basic idea is that it is our own mental processes, rather than the inconsiderate actions or statements of others, that unsettle us. For instance, Marshall Rosenberg—the architect of the otherwise astute popular psychology of nonviolent communication—boldly claims that "the cause of anger lies in our own thinking," adding that, if we are to contribute to peaceful relating, we must learn "to divorce the other person from any responsibility for our anger."

I understand that the objective of this kind of reasoning is to empower us so that we do not hand over the control of our emotional welfare to others. And it is designed to teach us to empathize with the deep needs and feelings of others, so that we come to understand that their hurtful actions are often motivated by their own pain. At the same time, anyone with even a modicum of awareness of how power functions in both social and intimate relationships will recognize how easy it is to twist this outlook to condone abusive behavior. When accountability resides with the recipient rather than the perpetrator of malicious deeds or statements, it is all too easy to evade responsibility by blaming the injured party. This is in fact one of the oldest stratagems of both racist and misogynistic hegemonies. Consequently, if the Ku Klux Klan burns a cross on my yard and I get angry, I am not going to accept the idea that I am the sole cause of my own anger. If my boyfriend beats me, my date rapes me, or my husband ridicules me, I am not going to let anyone tell me that my interpretative processes are fully responsible for my hurt feelings. There are circumstances where others—including our loved ones—behave cruelly and callously. Carrying the responsibility for their actions and statements in such cases would only play into the hands of power structures that have historically rendered some lives agonizing while simultaneously justifying various social and intimate atrocities.

Riding the Turbulence

When I propose that we may sometimes unwittingly trigger behaviors in our partner that are not typical of him, I am therefore not in the least bit implying that we should shoulder responsibility for his insensitive or thoughtless conduct. And I am not suggesting that we should allow him to shift the blame and hold us accountable for relationship problems that may be generated by his own lack of compassion, responsiveness, sincerity, or emotional maturity. I am not saying that we should tolerate our partner's arrogance, or meekly acquiesce when he treats us in patronizing or disrespectful ways. I am merely pointing out that it may at times be difficult for us to read the situation accurately and to determine why the repetition compulsion gets set in motion. It may be impossible for us to draw an interpretative link between our present lover and the people, including our parents, we have loved in the past.

Under these conditions, our best course of action may be to concede that when two individuals come together in a romantic alliance, they are more or less guaranteed to arouse each other's deep-seated unconscious patterns. And the more intimate the relationship, the more likely this is to happen. After all, the person we most love is also the person we let closest to ourselves. He or she is, by definition, someone who wields considerable power over us, and doubly so if we are hoping for some sort of redemption. From this perspective, the idea that we could somehow escape the repetition compulsion might be largely unrealistic. A more prudent approach might be to acknowledge that the compulsion is likely to complicate matters at some point. It might be wise to see it as an emotional "given" that we are bound to confront if we want our relationship to endure. That way, instead of wasting our energies on fighting the inevitable, we can focus on building a romantic rapport that is flexible enough to ride the turbulence caused by the compulsion. I am in fact tempted to say that those who expect their relationships to remain completely harmonious may inadvertently be setting themselves up for disillusionment. In contrast, those who see moments of disharmony as an intrinsic component of love increase their chances for genuine intimacy.

Because the manner in which two psyches and life histories intermingle remains opaque at best, we cannot explain why some people bring out the best in us, whereas others bring out the worst. And why some relationships flourish against all odds whereas others fall apart despite our most sincere efforts is an enigma that we will never be able to fully penetrate. Unconscious repetitions can lead to inexplicable relationship failures, malfunctions, and confused endings. Lovers can, for instance, be perennially out of sync with each other or with the timing of their emotional openness. One party arrives at an emotional junction, awaits the other with an escalating degree of impatience, and finally departs so as to salvage his sanity and self-respect. When the other, having gathered the necessary courage and clarity, at long last arrives, she will find no one waiting for her. While the first party misses out on love because he acts too fast, the second misses out because she acts too slowly. Neither is to blame. Yet both are responsible.

It can be difficult to decide how to proceed when we are faced with such repetitions. If a relationship is causing us distress, is it best to admit defeat and call for a swift separation so as to prevent further damage? Is the most constructive course of action to protect our integrity at all costs? Or does our commitment to our partner demand our willingness to work through repetitions in the hope that we may eventually reach a clearing beyond them? Does love ask us to stay present to relationship dilemmas even when we feel (re)traumatized by them? Or does it entail knowing when to cut our losses and move on?

It is impossible to give a definitive answer to such questions. There is no romantic relationship that is entirely devoid of crises. Consequently, much depends on the strength of devotion between the lovers, as well as on the composition of the problems themselves. Certain issues are worth addressing because we sense that on the other side of them reside growth and increased aliveness. Others present only energy-draining and mind-numbing cul-de-sacs. And what makes things doubly confusing is that it is frequently not possible to tell the difference between a problem that merits our time and effort, and a situation, or a lover, that is toxic and destructive. It can, in other words, be hard to distinguish between an opportunity for mutual enrichment and an abusive or codependent relationship.

The situation is further complicated by the fact that the repetition compulsion can drive us to irrational efforts to control our relationship. Particularly when we have not yet learned to handle the repetition, it can be tempting to try to contain it by manipulating our partner's actions. For instance, when we find ourselves confronting circumstances that remind us of some prior catastrophe, we might attempt to prevent its recurrence by restricting our partner's freedom. Or we might seek to defuse an ominous scenario by imposing boundaries on it. The more something in our psyches screams that we do not, once again, want a particular outcome, the more likely we are to erect artificial limits that are intended to foreclose that outcome. Unfortunately, our efforts are typically futile. Even if we manage to fend off the dreaded conclusion for the time being, it is likely to materialize at a later point. A contrived solution—one that does not reflect the reality of our relationship—will only hold temporarily. All of our exertions will therefore not guarantee the outcome we want. They will merely postpone (and thereby add sting to) the one we do not want.

Managing the Repetition

Managing unconscious repetitions is difficult and other professional help is required. However, it may be possible, under auspicious conditions, to slowly fashion a better relational configuration. To borrow from Lear, we may over time be able to forge a space for "the possibility of new possibilities"—for life directions and emotional scenarios that might have formerly seemed untenable to us. A litmus test for whether a particular relationship is worth an investment of this kind might be the eagerness of both partners to work through the repetition. A one-sided state of affairs where one partner is seeking change while the other is obstinately digging in his or her heels may not deserve the same dedication as one where both are devoted to bringing about a more gratifying reality. But even here, the line is blurry because it may be exactly the stubbornness of the reluctant partner that is most in need of being worked through.

It is not possible for any of us to entirely break our repetition compulsions. Because our present is always influenced by the experiences of the past, none of us can escape the fate-defining power of our history. But this should not prevent us from developing a more judicious relationship to the recurring patterns that haunt our existence; it should not keep us from doing our best to decode the ways our present actions and responses are propelled by the persistent phantoms of the past. After all, we can begin to modify our patterns only if we first develop enough self-awareness to accurately identify their distinctive profile. We unfortunately cannot accomplish this overnight, for transforming our unconscious patterns into a more resilient emotional constellation is a slow and at times torturous process. Indeed, it could be said to be a life-time occupation—something we can diligently work at but never definitively attain. But this does not mean that it does not warrant our earnest effort.

Working through unconscious patterns is worth the trouble because the more familiar we are with such patterns, the better we are able to pinpoint the part we play in the crafting of our emotional destinies. Rather than feeling perpetually persecuted by a brutal or uncaring world, we come to accept a measure of responsibility for the contours of our lives. As I have already stressed, in saying this I do not wish to discount those instances when the world actually does treat us in a brutal or uncaring fashion. Such instances are by no means a figment of our imagination. Nevertheless, it is helpful to identify the myriad ways in which we contribute to our destiny, if only by consistently selecting lovers who are unable to appreciate what we have to offer, or by accepting interpersonal dynamics that are not good for us. In short, being cognizant of our unconscious blueprints allows us to make more informed relationship choices, thereby leading to a higher degree of self-responsibility.

A greater familiarity with our unconscious patterns also helps us treat others more responsibly. In the same way that I am not going to concede that my anger at someone else's hurtful behavior is entirely my own doing, I am not going to claim—as someone like Marshall Rosenberg would prefer me to—that I am not in any way responsible for the feelings of others. The fact that the feelings of others ultimately arise from their own mental processes rather than from my actions does not alter the fact that, as an adult, I have enough emotional intelligence to be able to anticipate the impact of my actions. Even though I can never predict the responses of others entirely correctly, and even though I may at times be completely off the mark, in most cases I am able to make a ballpark estimate of how my actions are going to percolate in the inner life of others. If I cheat on my partner, I may not be able to foresee whether he will feel angry or sad (or both). But I will know for sure that he will not feel happy, loved, pleasantly surprised, or appreciated. If I tell my son that he is incompetent, disparage my friend, make a racist comment to a colleague, or say something mean to a student, I may not be able to guess at their exact sentiments, but I will know that they will not be feeling great or cared-for. And to the degree that I too do these things despite my understanding that they will wound others, I am fully responsible for their feelings. To pretend otherwise is to fall into bad faith.

Those (Rosenberg included) who advocate the idea that we should not hold ourselves responsible for the feelings of others tend to argue that worrying about how others might feel as a result of our actions or statements is too exhausting—that it does not contribute to our ability to lead an inspired existence. Alternatively, the reasoning is that acting out of obligation rather than out of spontaneous generosity is counterproductive because we end up resenting those we feel responsible for. This line of thinking is quite seductive, for undoubtedly many of us would like to ease the burden of our obligations and to lead an inspired life. But it can also serve as a front for emotional and ethical complacency. It can be used as a justification for egotistical and self-centered behavior, so that doing what inspires us equals doing whatever we happen to feel like doing, regardless of its cost to others.

In addition, the fact that women have traditionally been better tutored at emotional intelligence than men should make us a bit wary of arguments that imply that such intelligence is overrated—that we should stop worrying about how our actions and statements impact others and instead devote our energies to doing only what inspires us. Indeed, one of the most striking characteristics of popular psychological approaches that preach "inspiration" as the pinnacle of enlightenment is that the banal philosophies of life they advocate ("the only person who can hurt you is you," "you are fully responsible for your own well-being," "it is your own response, rather than the actions of others, that matters," etc.) sound suspiciously like the justifications of abusive lovers who do their best to avoid taking responsibility for their wounding behavior. Such lovers habitually try to turn the tables by convincing their partners that they are the root cause of their own pain—that if they learned to better control their reactions, they would not be so devastated. Against this backdrop, the quest for "inspiration" promoted by many popular psychologies can become an excuse for the most brutal conduct imaginable, offering a convenient rationalization for those who like to slide out of interpersonal accountability.

Human life is extremely complicated. It entails aspects that inspire us, and others that do not (as a matter of fact, if we invariably did what inspires us, after a while we would not be able to recognize inspiration for what it is). And it entails responsibilities that are not always easy to undertake, and that we sometimes find awfully exhausting. Working in a factory or a processing plant is exhausting, yet countless people do it. Getting up in the middle of the night to clear the snow off highways is exhausting, yet people (thankfully!) do it. Caring for children is exhausting, yet many people choose to do it. Likewise, worrying about the feelings of others may be exhausting, yet sometimes it is our responsibility to do so. Although there may be some people in the world who are privileged enough to do only what they feel inspired to do, most of us end up doing a lot of things that are not particularly spirit-lifting. And this may not always be such a bad thing. It is life, after all.

One of the most damaging aspects of the repetition compulsion is that the more it absorbs us, the more likely we are to fail at basic emotional intelligence. In other words, the more we ignore the power of the past to speak in the present, the more we risk abdicating our interpersonal accountability; we risk acting out on impulse, without pausing to think about the consequences of our actions. In contrast, when we take an active interest in the ways in which the unconscious guides our behavior, we increase our capacity to adequately care for those we love. This does not mean that we should try to tame or discipline our unconscious, for this would ultimately be a wasted effort. Nonetheless, the more connected we are to our recurring patterns, the more consistently we are able to catch ourselves whenever these patterns threaten to pull us into rigid networks of behavior that injure others; the more we "own" our unconscious as our personal liability, the more responsibly we are able to treat those closest to us. This kind of responsibility does not exhaust us but, quite the contrary, carves a passageway to more inspired relational possibilities. In this sense, there is no contradiction between our responsibility to others and our ability to feel inspired. Instead, the former is a precondition of the latter.

The more curious we are about our unconscious patterns, the easier it is for us to revise our romantic lives so that new relational plots and scenarios become available to us. When we start to amend the manner in which we interact with the world as a structure of interpersonal possibility, we may come to see that we have more options—that the field of possibilities is wider—than we are accustomed to think. When we expand the domain of what we consider emotionally attainable in our lives, we more or less automatically open a space for more ingenuous, authentic, relaxed, and playful modes of relating. Even when we cannot change the external world, we can modify the ways in which we relate to this world, and in this fashion, indirectly, the ways in which the world responds to us. We can over time rewrite the patterns of passion that motivate the choices we make, as well as the actions we take, in our most intimate relationships.

[3]

The Sliver of Eternity

If love is so full of illusions and painful repetitions, why do we want it so badly? The simple answer—one that this chapter is intended to complicate—is that we want it because it gives rise to an unparalleled sensation of self-awakening. Through love, a sliver of eternity, of what appears magical and awe-inspiring, inserts itself into our ordinary existence. We feel as if we had been touched by a magnificent force that lends nobility to our lives, lifting us to an existential sphere that feels more elevated, more meaningful, than the one we normally inhabit.

Under usual conditions, we tend to glide through the world without paying much attention to its intricate texture. Meeting the demands of the day often requires that we temporarily disregard our surroundings; we procure our everyday efficiency by suspending our connection to those parts of the world that do not serve our practical concerns. One of the amazing powers of love is that it offers a potent remedy to such carelessness. When we fall in love, dimensions of the world that have remained blurry or marginal suddenly click into focus for us. Neglected aspects of our environment clamor for notice. Facets of life that we normally ignore take on a heightened significance. Through an openness to those shades of our surroundings that usually remain eclipsed, we become keenly attentive to the myriad details of our lives.

While our ordinary preoccupations take place in the world, they also, in some ways, distance us from it. They distract us from the *worldness* of the world, as it were, because they are designed to allow us to make use of the world rather than to become fully and passionately immersed within its folds. In this sense, navigating the routine tasks and liabilities of life is not at all the same thing as being in touch with the pulse of the world. What is so wonderful about love is that it reconnects us to this pulse. It cuts through the din of our regular concerns so that we feel uncompromisingly real, aligned with the roundedness and timelessness of being. Yet we also feel firmly anchored in the here and now, embedded in the concrete materiality of the world. In a way, we are able to touch the sublime without ever leaving the world behind.

There are of course other experiences besides falling in love that summon us to this kind of acute vigilance. These can be as uncomplicated as inhaling the invigorating crispness of autumn air, observing the intricate design of snowflakes on a window pane, or running our fingers over the velvety surface of a fine piece of paper. Or they can be as complicated as trying to intuit and respond to a friend's pain or apprehension. What such experiences have in common, however, is that they invite us to perceive the world more carefully. They ask us to slow down and proceed with more deliberation than we usually do. Sometimes they enable us to find value in something that appears entirely banal. Other times they allow us to recognize beauty within what is seemingly devoid of it. In this manner, they ensure the liveliness of our spirit, fending off states of inner stagnation. They assure that we do not get completely buried under the morass of our practical concerns. Like eros, they carry us to an enchanted place that is filled with intimations of eternity, giving rise to a robust sense of being part of something that exceeds the purely commonplace or circumstantial.

The Human and the Divine

In this—as in so many other things—we have a great deal to learn from Plato, who already saw eros as a means of approaching a realm of uncorrupted truth and beauty that otherwise remains largely inaccessible to us. He advanced a two-tiered conception of the universe by distinguishing between an invisible realm of divine perfection and the inherently flawed terrain of human life. While the divine realm embodied pure and immutable ideals, the human domain was composed of defective copies or imitations of these ideals. In this context, the task of the seeker of enlightenment was to ascend, as far as he could, the (intangible and spiritual) ladder that led from the realm of human materiality to the sphere of divine ideality. His mission was to penetrate the worldly veil of illusions and appearances amidst which humans lived so as to gain a glimpse of the more exalted reality that was obscured by this veil. And Plato did not hesitate to suggest that eros was one of the most effective means of accomplishing this task.

Plato explained that before our soul got encased in the material vessel of our body, it enjoyed the company of the gods. Having been asked to drink from the river of Lethe (of forgetfulness) prior to settling into its human host, it does not explicitly recall this, yet it retains an intuitive connection to the celestial domain it has lost. More specifically, the feverish desire we experience when we fall in love signifies that our soul is yearning to rise to the transcendent realm from which it has been exiled by its earthly existence. The fact that the person we love incarnates ideal beauty on Earth stimulates our longing to reunite with divine beauty. We may not be consciously aware of this nebulous affiliation between earthly and divine beauty.

Yet our insistent craving for the company of our beloved is a sign that our soul is enthusiastically preparing for its upward flight toward the incandescent province of divine splendor.

In one of his most famous similes, Plato portrays the soul as a winged entity awaiting the reviving jolt of eros. He specifies that while earthly existence causes the feathers on the surface of the soul's wings to wither away from lack of use, falling in love softens and revitalizes the passages from which the feathers grow, allowing new feathers to shoot. The strange agitation that we feel in love is thus, metaphorically speaking, an indication that our soul is refeathering its wings so as to better soar to the heights. Plato depicts this state of the soul as one of mingled pleasure and pain that renders us irrational, tumultuous, and even a bit insane. As he posits, "the soul of a man who is beginning to grow his feathers has the same sensation of pricking and irritation and itching as children feel in their gums when they are just beginning to cut their teeth."

The restlessness of the lover is hence expressive of the soul's impatience to recapture a divine domain. Eros, in a sense, bridges the human and the divine. Plato's parable implies that if there is something about human life that makes it difficult for us to remain cognizant of the transcendent dimensions of life, eros insists on animating those dimensions; it insists that we look beyond the daily grind. The fact that we may not be able to name or accurately describe this experience does not dilute its power to move us. In the same way that the wings of the soul swell with the regrowth of feathers, love makes us feel as if we were able to reach beyond the familiar topography of our everyday reality. We attain a stirring sensation of coming to our own, arriving, as it were, at a loftier sense of life's possibilities.

We do not need to believe in divinity in the sense that Plato is talking about to grasp what he is getting at. We know that eros calls us to realms of self-experience that make us feel more actualized. However, what is perhaps less obvious (and therefore noteworthy) about this is that we tend to purchase our sense of self-actualization at the price of our social identities. That is, eros rewards us only to the extent that we are willing to temporarily sideline, or ever suspend, the socially intelligible persona through which we customarily negotiate our place in the world. It carries us into a quasi-mythological domain where the normal matrix of social relations no longer applies, effectively fissuring the façade that demarcates our personal boundaries. As a consequence, our most treasured moments of transcendence—those moments when the sliver of eternity manages to touch our spirit—are also often piercing experiences of surrender and self-loss.

The Nick of Time

Oddly enough, the dissolution of social identity that characterizes moments of erotic surrender does not connote submission or victimization. Even though such moments can make us feel temporarily "seized," "erased," or "taken over" by a force more powerful than us, they do not make us feel mortified or defeated. Quite the contrary, we tend to feel rejuvenated and more immediately connected to ourselves. During such moments, time stands still so that the usual distinctions between past, present, and future cease to function. We fall outside of time, as it were. We exist in a space of infinity, complete and fully meaningful in itself. Eros, in a deep sense, arrests time's unremitting movement into an instant of timelessness. Or, to express the matter in the words of the contemporary philosopher Elizabeth Grosz, eros represents the emergence of what is "untimely" within the timely, epitomizing a "cut" or a "nick" that punctures time's incessant motion by a pure moment of stillness. This explains why it allows us to feel fulfilled and in touch with the most profound layers of our being.

In the same way that our spirits might climb at the sight of something sublime or strikingly beautiful, the experience of being captivated by eros feels self-enhancing. This of course does not guarantee that we will not get wounded. In fact, given that erotic surrender by definition exposes our soft underbelly to the person we love, the potential for hurt and abuse is ever-present. By opening ourselves to eros on this fundamental level—by inviting another person to dwell within our being in ways that are potentially explosive—we inevitably trade away our claim on security. Our culture does its best to lull us into an innocent complacency about eros by saturating us with images of light-hearted romance and happy endings. Yet anyone who has ever truly loved knows that even the most gratifying love affairs are at times wrought with anxiety, hesitation, apprehension, and moments of utter helplessness.

In the realm of eros, exposure to the possibility of pain is the flip side of transcendence. As a result, whenever we choose to make a leap of faith into the unknown that eros represents, we are never far from disaster. It is hardly surprising, then, that many of us learn to view love as a threat to our viability as sovereign and self-sufficient creatures. It is no wonder that we learn to skid its fragile surface with a nimble-footed lightness that is intended to protect us from its lures and treacherous trapdoors. After all, how do we know that we will manage to withstand the destabilizations of eros? How can we be sure that we will be able to reemerge from experiences of self-disintegration with our identities intact? What assurance do we have that we will be resilient enough to reclaim solid ground afterwards?

If one of the goals of social existence is to establish the necessary boundaries between self and others, eros strives to demolish such boundaries, hearkening back to those earliest stages of life when the basic distinction between the self and the world was not yet entirely established. This is one reason that eros calls for a sinuous interplay between the structured (social) and unstructured (asocial) elements of our being; it demands a sustained ability to move back and forth between these two (seemingly incompatible) realms. Some of us find this easier than others. Many of us know that we are able to embrace disjointed states of self-experience without thereby imperiling our coherent selves. We remain confident that we will be able to recover our more structured identities relatively rapidly. And we understand that being able to embrace archaic forms of connectedness feeds our ongoing aptitude for transformation by making us feel ardently engaged in our lives. Some of us, however, refuse love's summons because we find the prospect of teetering on the verge of self-loss too daunting.

It may well be that we need a fairly secure sense of our personal boundaries to be able to benefit from states of surrender and self-dissolution. Though some of us are kept from such experiences by personal boundaries that are too rigid—too tightly defended and impermeable—others may resist them because our boundaries are too flimsy. When we are not entirely sure where the edges of our personality reside, it may be doubly difficult for us to allow these edges to disband, however fleetingly. In such cases, the biggest reward of eros may well be to illustrate that there are ways to let go of our self-certainty without falling irrevocably. By this I mean quite simply that the more we practice giving ourselves over to erotic experience, the more assured we grow in the knowledge that we will not lose our footing permanently. If the rest of our culture tends to equate surrender with powerlessness, eros teaches us that it is possible to relinquish control without being irredeemably weakened or derailed.

The Fall Into Tenderness

The most common way to understand erotic surrender is to think about soul-scorching sex. But there are other modalities of surrender that may be less self-evident. The philosopher Luce Irigaray, for example, proposes that sometimes we reach a space of surrender through something as simple as our lover's devoted caress. Such a caress is a gentle gesture that allows us to shed the practical layers of our daily reality so as to access a more transcendent existential frequency. According to this formulation, transcendence is not a function of the soul's flight into a higher realm, as it is in Plato's rendering. Nor is it necessarily an experience of timelessness whereby we exit the chronological sequence of our lives. Rather, it is a fall into tenderness that allows us to become more intensely embedded within the sensuous folds of the passing moment, and particularly of our own materiality. The caress seeks no reward beyond the tactile realities of the world. Yet it is not mundane. It effectively detaches us from the routine concerns that normally fill our consciousness.

The fast-paced and overstimulating tempo of modern life can shut down vital aspects of self-experience. We can become so focused on trying to achieve social and material insignias of success, so swept up in the currents of consumer culture, and so harassed by the incessant demands of daily survival that we lose touch with the more archaic layers of our being; we "forget" how to relax into our minds and bodies. Alternatively, we can become so immersed in the pragmatic responsibilities of our existence that we develop an overly rational approach to the process of living, thereby neglecting the more intuitive, spontaneous, or emotionally resonant densities of life. Over time, we can begin to feel psychologically and physically indigent. Against this backdrop, a lover's caress can restore our capacity to listen to the messages of our interiority and body alike. It can induce us to pay more attention to what might be laboring for expression from within the foundations of our being.

In Irigaray's terms, a lover's caress is an invitation to meet the world in a way that is more mindful and contemplative than our habitual goal-oriented existence. As she states, the caress is an "an awakening to a life different from the arduous everyday." If day-to-day life often draws us into its utilitarian concerns so tightly that we come to overlook our most rudimentary needs, the caress recalls us to a more restful mode of being. By cutting through the polite structures of sociality, and by releasing us from the strenuous requirements of the workday, it enables us to enter a more serene bodily and emotional space. It slows down the rhythm of our lives so that we can gain entry into sediments of our being that under normal conditions remain masked; it helps us connect with parts of ourselves that tend to get lost in the frenzy of our public lives. Ideally, we emerge from its recesses amplified, with our capacity to confront the challenges of the world rehabilitated.

Everyday life can make us feel besieged and overwhelmed in part because it exacts a more or less habitual denial of the body and its desires. Many of us are used to thinking about the body as what keeps us from being sufficiently focused on our practical pursuits. It gets tired and needy. And it distracts us from our "higher" goals and preoccupations. Consequently, we frequently develop an antagonistic, and sometimes even an overtly hostile, relationship to our body. We may do our best to ignore its demands whenever these threaten to undermine our efficiency. At times, we may even feel ashamed of it, particularly when it does not measure up to our ideals of beauty or endurance. Under such circumstances, a loving caress restores our bodily integrity, allowing us to experience a roundness of embodied self-presence that, momentarily at least, heals the rift between us and our own materiality.

Every now and then we even find a way to transfer the soothing effects of the caress into the commotion that makes up the rest of our lives. Even as the caress gradually fades away, its trace lingers on as an enduring mark of bodily attentiveness that infuses our ordinary occupations with an elusive yet luscious tranquility. In effect, once we have allowed ourselves to experience such a moment of richness, we can use it to evaluate other aspects of our lives. It can become a prism through which we scrutinize our daily existence so as to ensure that we do not settle for what is merely convenient, but rather put our passion behind those goals, actions, and relational dynamics that allow us to stay connected with ourselves, as well as with those we love. It can act as our private escort beyond the morass of the mundane social interactions that tend to fill our lives with trivial (yet exhausting) activity.

Social interactions invariably entail an exchange of emotional, psychic, and physical energies. While many of these exchanges invigorate us, others consume our being. In addition, exchanges that are cutting or malicious denigrate us, bordering on soul-murder and subduing the voice of our inner giant. As a consequence, we need ways to counteract the expenditures of sociality. We need ways to keep our lives from sliding into defensive patterns of relating to the world. And we need ways to protect our psyches from the sterile solutions offered by much of mass culture. The caress can help us in this regard because it allows us to regather those fragments of ourselves that have been scattered around by the pressures of living. It offers a valuable reprieve from the ordeals of social exchange.

The caress of course is also a form of social exchange in the sense that it involves two individuals with distinctive personalities. However, while most other forms of social exchange ask us to activate our public persona, the caress implores us to "return" to ourselves beyond the realm of collective categories and classifications. It encourages us to dip into the least socially regimented echelons of our character, thereby activating what is most peculiarly "us" outside of the demands of collective negotiation. Indeed, one reason that the caress replenishes us is that it allows us to circumvent the usual currencies of social exchange. Within its cocoon, there is no need to rationalize, reflect, deliberate, or talk things through. Instead, there is a subtle and insubstantial flow of nonverbal communications that bespeaks a certain porosity of being. Through the caress, we are able to cross the permeable boundaries between self and other effortlessly and without the slightest sense of violation.

The caress opens up horizons of experience that we could not attain independently of our partner. It is a way of coming together in a sheltered space of mutual reassurance. And although it takes place on the surface of the body, it can reverberate within the deepest indentations of our being. It responds to our need to be reached and understood in a profound way, as who we are beneath the refined veneer that we display to the world. We can in fact feel terribly forlorn when we sense that our partner fails to touch the "real" of our being—that he or she is merely enamored of our public façade. In contrast, the loving caress bears witness to those aspects of our being that we typically conceal from others. In this sense, whether we experience the caress as a transcendent moment, or simply as a means of melting away the tensions of the day, it galvanizes realms of interiority that cannot be reached by logic alone.

There are individuals who are exceptionally good at facilitating moments of surrender. They offer an evocative presence that allows us to fall into a state of self-fragmentation without triggering our anxiety about not being able to find our way back to our social identity. Their silent yet attentive presence builds a foundation for a connection that is neither impinging nor intrusive, but rather calmly embracing. Because there is a finely woven reliability to the care they provide, they manage to create a peaceful refuge of intimacy that effortlessly removes the clutter of our minds and bodies alike. As a result, they invite unscripted and unself-conscious pieces of our interiority to make their way into the open. They may even allow petrified forms of pain to play themselves out in the empathetic space between self and other. In this way, they make it possible for us to begin a tentative conversation with dissociated or prohibited facets of our being, thereby facilitating our continued capacity for personal renewal—for what philosophers have called the process of "becoming."

The Process of Becoming

The process of becoming ensures that our identities are never fixed once and for all but remain in constant evolution. This process is what lends our existence its distinctively human character by granting us the ability to self-reflexively (and repeatedly) inquire into the possibilities of our future. Many of us enter this process with a degree of deliberation, asking ourselves how we can best meet the needs of ourselves and others, what kinds of goals are worth pursuing, which existential paths grant us the greatest degree of aliveness, and what the most dexterous course of action in a specific situation might be.

In this manner, we strive to develop our own distinctive art of living, making a commitment to foster the singular "spirit" that allows us to feel like "ourselves." We dedicate our lives to cultivating the characteristic inner lexicon that determines how we reside in the world.

Our answers to life-defining questions change over time. Because there is no way to halt the interplay of question and answer, there is in principle no end to the process of becoming. Indeed, even when we actively resist this process—even when we choose to lead more or less haphazard lives—we cannot entirely arrest its momentum, for it is the very essence of human life to be in a continual flux. Though it is not necessarily the case that a conscious effort to fashion an identity results in a more rewarding life than one where no such effort has been made, it would be difficult for any of us to completely escape the realization that our lives are by definition unresolved and therefore open to constant reconfiguration; it would be difficult to avoid seeing that there is always room for refinement. Yet it is tempting to try to overlook this. It is tempting to neglect the interplay of question and answer that epitomizes human existence, for doing so can reduce our apprehension about having to make explicit decisions about the parameters of our lives.

Our identities are rich with potentialities that we can either pick up or ignore, that we can either materialize or fail to materialize. One of our biggest challenges, then, is to resist getting caught up in complacent forms of being, for it is when we become too attached to any one incarnation of ourselves that we forfeit our capacity for regeneration—that we give up on our process of becoming. Sadly, our everyday lives make it almost impossible to avoid such habitual attachments because they usually demand that we privilege one version of ourselves over all others, and that we do so repeatedly, until all alternatives fade into the background and become increasingly difficult to discern. In other words, our daily existence is in many ways designed to seduce us into a deeply complacent understanding of our life's mission; it is designed to exhaust the momentum of transformation that lends vitality to our being.

This is the case in part because our everyday lives are founded on a fairly coherent and well-established psychic structure. This structure is reassuring because it enables us to function effectively and to some extent anticipate the outlines of our future. Yet it is also limiting in the sense that it automatically eliminates or suppresses elements that do not comfortably fit within its confines. Like most other structures, it works by simplifying and streamlining, by molding new ingredients to correspond to preexisting patterns, as well as by excluding ingredients that resist such molding. As a result, although it provides a measure of existential consistency, it simultaneously exacts a high price by compelling us to relinquish dimensions of ourselves that do not serve the whole. We are, as it were, obliged to give up some aspects of ourselves so as to allow others to thrive. According to this perspective, our identities gain predictability at the expense of those features that appear to interfere with or confuse the intelligibility of our lives; the clarity we seem to have about ourselves demands a lot of sacrifices.

Some of these sacrifices, while perhaps forgotten on the conscious level, continue to live on as unconscious components of our interiority. They persist as melancholy pockets of psychic and affective possibility that have not been properly mourned and that, consequently, still lurk in the shadowy crevices of our being. One reason that eros moves us so intensely—that it feels so transcendent—is that it extends a generous summons to these components; it invites what has been stifled, estranged, undervalued, and unarticulated back into our lives. By encouraging us to recuperate splintered aspects of our being, it reminds us of, and brings us in touch with, what we have had to renounce in order to claim a place in the world. It is therefore no wonder that it makes us feel as if a sliver of eternity was suddenly announcing itself within our mundane reality. On this view, we covet romantic experiences not only because they bring us pleasure, but because they animate as-of-yet-uncharted potentialities of our interiority; they elevate us to otherwise unattainable levels of self-awareness.

The Reinvention of Identity

The fact that our identities are never complete implies that self-fashioning is a task we must resume time and again. Fortunately for us, romantic relationships hold an especially strong promise for the concretization of embryonic potentialities because they contain an almost interminable string of moments when we are called to renegotiate our identities. Though the particulars of our selfhood are dependent on our interactions with more or less everyone we encounter, romantic attachments are particularly likely to induce us to actively take up the ever-renewed challenge of deciding how we wish to live. This is because we cannot sustain an intimate relationship without considerable psychic restructuring; we cannot invite a lover to share our lives without being willing to redesign our inner universe. Every new alliance, and every modification of an already existing one, offers us an opportunity for self-cultivation. In this sense, loving another person is not merely a matter of discovering and appreciating who he or she is, but also of determining who and what we can become in relation to him or her. In short, our lovers can serve as catalysts for the reinvention of our identities.

In chapter 1, I outlined the dangers of using lovers to prop up our narcissistic quest for self-completion. The dynamic I am talking about here is different not only because the gifts of relationality are, potentially at least, reciprocal in the sense that we can accelerate our lover's process of becoming as much as he or she accelerates ours, but also because we are not asking our lover to reflect back to us a static (and flattering) image of ourselves. Rather, we are asking him or her to promote our ability to connect with sacrificed parts of ourselves so that we can, over time, craft ourselves into more intricate beings. By empowering us to surpass the limitations of the various structures—rules, regulations, and self-imposed restrictions—that we have come to take for granted over the years, romantic love makes it possible for us to begin to work toward a new kind of self-relation. If we are lucky, it reignites the spark that lends our personality its inimitable specificity.

This explains why we sometimes find ourselves hurled into a state of profound longing reminiscent of the agitation that the soul, according to Plato, experiences when it is regrowing its feathers; it explains why eros makes us want to spread our wings in the Platonic sense. In Plato's account, eros offers the soul a glimpse of the divine radiance it has lost. In the account I have advanced, it gives us a taste of what is missing from our lives, reminding us of what we have had to give up in order to evolve into the person we currently are. If Irigaray's caress offers us a soothing model of transcendence, my quasi-Platonic model asks us to think deeply not only about who we are, but also about what we would ideally like to become; it motivates us to realize ourselves on a more multidimensional level. In the best of circumstances, these two models complement each other, allowing us to work toward a fuller understanding of the various ways in which relationality is a key component of self-cultivation.

It may be worth noting that self-cultivation through relationships has traditionally been viewed as a "feminine" approach. If de Beauvoir warned women against overinvesting themselves in romance, it is because historically women were trained to do so. While men were expected to make their mark in the world through various forms of creative, intellectual, political, military, or financial achievement, women were, until recently, seen as the primary guardians of relationality. This clarifies why relationality, in Western culture at least, has had to play second fiddle to other forms of self-actualization, so that we often do not consider the full existential implications of what it means to interact with others in loving ways. Until the last century, philosophers (with the exception of Plato, Kierkegaard, and a handful of others) tended to relegate romantic relationships to the margins of their thinking. As a consequence, although we certainly celebrate the more sappy and superficial aspects of romance in our songs, movies, magazines, and wedding rituals, our cultural heritage has not accustomed us to recognize how fundamental intimate alliances can be to the overall scheme of our lives.

We also tend to downplay what I have chosen to accentuate in this book, namely, that, as a form of self-cultivation, relationality is far from straightforward. This makes it all the more crucial to pay attention to what kinds of lovers we let into our world. As I pointed out in the introduction, and as I have tried to elaborate in this chapter, the people we invite into our lives influence our basic sense of who we are. There are those who trigger our suppressed aggressions and resentments. And there are others who deplete us, sapping our strength and sending us into a spiral of negativity and self-doubt. In later chapters, I will illustrate that even such experiences may be spiritually or emotionally necessary for us in the sense that they can teach us valuable lessons about ourselves and about our patterns of relating. In this circuitous fashion, they may contribute to the density of our character as much as our more supportive relationships. Nonetheless, knowing how to select lovers who free, evoke, and illuminate the best parts of our interiority is essential for our ability to release our unique subjective idiom. As the psychoanalyst Christopher Bollas notes, there are people who serve as psychic keys that open doors to meaningful inner experience—to what he describes as "a form of lifting" that ushers us into "a new knowing of ourselves." Such lifting allows for a greater versatility of personal (and interpersonal) expression, thus greatly supporting our process of becoming.

If specific lovers captivate us more than others—if they consistently make us reach for that sliver of eternity—this may well be because they manage to mobilize those of our inner passions that matter to us the most. They meet our singularity with kindness and generosity, thereby providing an inspiring environment for the creative unfolding of our potentialities. Such lovers not only help us forge gratifying romantic alliances but also confirm that our emotional alertness, let alone our process of becoming, depends on our openness to others. Indeed, the moment we become impervious to the influence of others, we risk losing our inner elasticity. In this sense, it is our continued capacity to love and be loved that allows us to evolve over time. Though the perils of love can be formidable, too hesitant an approach to romance may in the long run be equally detrimental in causing us to atrophy inside. From this point of view, our faithfulness to love's summons means being willing to heed its invitation to continuous self-inquiry. It entails being willing to repeatedly question the habitual contours of our lives so that fresh existential configurations become possible for us. While there is no doubt that eros can at times feel overwhelming because it pulls us in life directions that are unfamiliar to us, our fidelity to it requires that we respect this pull.

[4]

The Midst of Life

Whether love seizes us without warning or catches up with us with premeditated softness, it ruptures the ordinary rhythm of our lives. The thrill of love arises in part precisely from this rupture. We enjoy being jolted out of the complacency of our everyday existence. We are eager to explore the mysterious opportunities of the soul that love awakens within us. And we are enthralled by the promise of emotional revitalization that eros represents. At the same time, the closer we come to a genuine connection with a lover, the more likely we are to resist love's summons. Sometimes we even reconcile ourselves to an uninspiring liaison because we are afraid that anything more fervent could get us irredeemably damaged; we give up some of our yearning for existential wonder in exchange for the relative security of tidy and lukewarm habits of intimacy. In this sense, one of the bitter paradoxes of life is that it is at times quite difficult for us to embrace the very passion that we crave; it is sometimes difficult for us to let the sliver of eternity enter our world.

One reason for this is that our culture emits a mixed message about love. On the one hand, we are taught that nothing in our lives can match the heady satisfaction of the kind of intimacy that melds two individuals into one—that creates an amorous alliance that surpasses the limitations of each of its participants. On the other, we are warned that the promises of love are deceptive at best, likely to mislead us in calamitous and heartbreaking ways; we are told to be on a vigilant lookout for the cruel snares of love. No wonder we are confused: we are advised to exercise caution toward the very thing that we are also most supposed to desire.

But our trepidation reaches beyond cultural conditioning. Few of us can say that love makes our lives less complicated. And many of us have been injured seemingly beyond repair. It is then hardly surprising that we often hesitate. Yet if we never risk ourselves—if we never take up the stirring call and reply of eros—we miss out on the furtive underworld of desire and ardency that comprises one of the most engaging riddles of human existence; we sidestep the enclave of spirit-rousing ambiguity that eros introduces to our lives. Sadly, the more we strive to curtail the daring flights of our romantic imagination, the more we deprive ourselves of emotional frequencies that confer an element of enchantment to our (otherwise often quite dreary) universe.

Romantic love invites us to live according to the momentum of our desire. I have already started to suggest that how we choose to respond to this invitation can, quite literally, determine our destiny. Whether we meet the challenges of love with courage, or whether we flee from them for fear of being devastated, our decision has far-reaching consequences for the rest of our lives. A premature retreat may render the world a more manageable place for us by removing a whole array of uncertainties. Yet, as we have seen, it also constricts the scope of our lives by shutting down emotional and existential pathways that only become available to us through love. A decisive step toward love, in contrast, might enable us to enter what the French philosopher Emmanuel Levinas eloquently describes as "the midst of life." It might allow us to step into the unstable current of our existence with a combination of ardor and dedication. And, under favorable conditions, it might even empower us to connect to the "truth" of our being.

The True Self

One of the best ways to understand what it means to feel connected to the "truth" of our being might be through a distinction that the famous British psychoanalyst D. W. Winnicott draws between our "true" and "false" self. The true self, according to Winnicott, possesses an existential suppleness that allows it to approach the practice of living—what I have portrayed as an ongoing process of becoming— with a measure of resourcefulness. The false self, in contrast, is a defensive structure that relates to the world in stiff and largely artificial ways. While this distinction might lead us to assume that the true self represents some sort of an innate core of selfhood that becomes corrupted by the false self, the matter is actually a lot more complicated. First of all, the true self is not a compilation of fixed attributes that would somehow, once and for all, determine who we are, but rather what guarantees our continuous aptitude for inner renewal. And, second, the false self is less an enemy of the true self than a protective shield against external trauma.

Winnicott explains that our inner agility is threatened whenever we feel assaulted by the outside world—whenever we feel traumatized either by our intimate relationships or by a wounding social context. Predictably enough, our usual response to such situations is to set up psychological barriers to protect ourselves against being violated. Such defensive barriers over time congeal into false self-presentations that make us feel reassuringly self-contained even as they gradually deprive us of our existential elasticity; we feel impermeable, and sometimes even invincible, without necessarily being aware of the ways in which we have relinquished our claim on a full-bodied life. As our true self slips into hiding behind the false one, we become more and more unyielding, more and more uncompromising, often alienating the people we most care about. Yet, ironically enough, the ultimate goal of the false self is to safeguard the continued viability of the true self in the face of external challenges. In this paradoxical fashion, the false self, though itself utterly incapable of emotional complexity, sustains our latent capacity for such complexity by ensuring that our true self does not get exploited to the point of total suffocation.

The purpose of the false self, then, is to assemble an impenetrable wall between the true self and the world so as to defend the dignity of the true self. In practice this means that we form an outer layer of personality—a "thick skin" or a "hardened shell"—that appears almost inanimate. We allow the part of ourselves that we present to the world to die, or at least to become so unresponsive as to give the impression of callous disregard for its surroundings. Our true self can in fact become so thoroughly masked by the defensive postures of the false self that others can no longer detect it at all. Instead, they relate to the false self, imagining this to be who we really "are." Indeed, because the false self functions effectively enough on many levels of daily life, it can sometimes deceive even the most intimate of companions. However, it fails to convince others in situations that presuppose a versatility of being. This is because it has lost its capacity to be at ease with itself; it has lost the openness to the adventure of loving and relating that allows us to maintain an adroit sense of self.

The tragedy of the false self, therefore, is that even if its solid armor of self-reliance manages to shelter the deeper layers of our being from injury, this armor simultaneously keeps us from forming a meaningful connection to the outside world. Sadly, the desperate exertions of the false self can make us feel even more false: shallow and devoid of purpose. Because the false self—sometimes for very good reasons—experiences the world as inherently hostile or impinging, it can become so fixated on sheer survival that we end up feeling that we have been drained of every drop of our humanity.

Sometimes we may even become so inundated by fear that we find it impossible to relax our restless hypervigilance even when we are not confronted by any immediate danger; we may remain on the defensive simply because we have learned to anticipate, as well as to brace ourselves against, trauma.

One of the most insidious components of trauma is that it makes it difficult for us to meet the world as a generous space of possibility. It damages not only the present (the moment when it is first inflicted), but also the future, in the sense that it robs us of our capacity for what Winnicott calls "creative living." However, Winnicott specifies that our aptitude for creative living can never be entirely destroyed—that although it can be compromised, it cannot ever be completely extinguished. Winnicott in fact insists that the distinction between creative and noncreative living is not categorical, but that we tend to vacillate between these two modalities. In other words, even when we fail to live creatively, we retain the intuition that we might be able to do so at some future point. As Winnicott observes, "In a tantalizing way many individuals have experienced just enough of creative living to recognize that for most of their time they are living uncreatively." Interestingly, then, the very fact that we often feel disconnected from our capacity for creative living—that we are aware that something is amiss in our lives—is a sign that we are still psychologically alive, that some untamed or unbroken part of us is still crying for recognition.

The Touch of Madness

We do not need to have a false self in the sense that Winnicott portrays it to profit from his analysis, for most of us resort to false self-presentations from time to time. One reason that falling in love can feel so healing and life-affirming is that it counters this tendency. It restores our capacity for inner spontaneity and creative living, thereby releasing the true self from its hiding place. It thus makes sense that many of us see love as a means of touching and being touched in ways that resonate with the "truth" of our being. As I have implied, this does not mean that love resurrects some sort of an immutable essence of personality that makes us who we are. Quite the contrary, being able to access the true self—in Winnicott's sense at least – enables us to better embrace the inconsistencies and sudden reversals of our lives. It ushers us into the midst of life precisely because it allows us to sustain the process of continual transformation that constitutes human existence.

In the previous chapter, I described the surrender to tenderness that is made possible by a lover's caress. This is one way in which we manage to create space for the true self in the midst of our daily existence. A lover's peaceful caress magically (albeit momentarily) erases forms of intrusive, vindictive, or overstimulating external reality, offering us a much-coveted respite from the myriad demands of the world. Through it, we fall into a state of repose where we do not need to exert ourselves in any way and where we do not need to uphold a polished or confident image. We allow our shield and armor (let alone our sword) to roll out of reach. In this manner, with the unspoken "permission" of our lover, we feel free to let our false self liquefy so that the true one can claim an existential foothold. This is one example of how a loving dynamic can revive our ability to connect with ourselves, and hence, over time, with others.

More generally speaking, there can be something uniquely rewarding about being liberated from the oppressive idea that we are only lovable to the degree that we manage to conceal the raw and defenseless dimensions of our being. Many of us yearn to be accepted despite, and perhaps even because of, the less than perfect inner universe that we inhabit. Because we do not want to discover one day that our lover does not know us at all—because we do not wish to be appreciated solely on the basis of the front we present to the world—we long to disclose what we usually hold back from others. It is therefore not surprising that we tend to feel a special connection to those who manage to animate the deepest creases of our being. Lovers who treat us with suitable sensitivity and thoughtfulness electrify our most compelling mythologies of self-actualization, with the result that we feel revitalized, as if tingling with new forms of life. This is an indication that whatever has been dead or subdued in us is gasping for air.

The flip side of this is that, in relating to our partner, we need to be prepared for the sharp points of personality that stick out of, and refuse to be disciplined into, smooth social enactments. We need to be prepared for the rough edges of his or her anxiety, disquiet, sorrow, or distress. As the contemporary critic Eric Santner posits, being able to connect to the uncanny singularity of another person's character means exposure not only to his thoughts, values, hopes, life history, and memories, but also to his unique "touch of madness." That is, we are asked to tolerate those aspects of the other that are somehow disquieting or disturbing to us—that might at times even cause us to wince and recoil. We are asked to honor the fact that, like us, our lover may occasionally find himself disoriented in the world. In the same way that our own singularity—the deepest "truth" of our being—conveys what cannot be fully domesticated by the protocols of sociality, the singularity of the person we love expresses something about the characteristic ways in which he finds himself bewildered, forlorn, or out of kilter.

The Flight from Passion

Many of us yearn for the kind of intimacy that inspires our true self. Yet, as I proposed in the beginning of this chapter, we sometimes end up fleeing from our most promising love affairs. We know that dropping our guard can be dangerous—that our longing for an authentic connection can sometimes lead to the mortification of the very part of ourselves that aspires to authenticity in the first place. And we also recognize that reclaiming traumatized dimensions of our interiority can take us within a striking distance of everything that we are doing our best to forget and foreclose. We understand that whenever we allow our true self to be penetrated, we risk shedding light into the cavern of our most hurtful secrets; we risk reviving unprocessed deposits of pain and grief. And so, in our panic, we can convince ourselves that the person we most love is not that important to us. We may even play power games in an attempt to reassure ourselves that he or she is more or less disposable, that we do not really care whether the relationship continues or not. In this way, we may end up being careless with the person who most merits our care.

This explains in part why we at times walk away from relationships that have the potential to be life-altering. Or why, if we choose to stick around, we frequently end up holding back or stringing our lover along without being able to make up our mind. What is colloquially called "commitment phobia" may on occasion have to do with the fact that our courage falters in the face of a profound connection. We tiptoe to the verge of the abyss but pull back because we are terrified of the uncertainties that meet us there. In such cases, the person who most consistently manages to defuse our defenses, and who would therefore most challenge and change us in the long run, is the one we push away because the stakes of awakening the true self seem too high. Sometimes we may even opt for another lover who seems safe and sensible, but who does not have the capacity to puncture the well-monitored borders of our false self. We end up settling for the "reasonable" comforts of a reliable relationship with someone with whom we are more or less compatible, but for whom we feel no real passion. We eliminate lovers who resonate with our most fundamental yearnings because these yearnings disturb us.

It does not help that we live in a culture that does its best to convince us of the naiveté of strong passions. On the one hand, we are encouraged to feel strongly about fairly superficial things such as designer clothes, flashy cars, the right vacations, speedy career advancement, or coloring the gray out of our hair. We in fact live amidst what the cultural critic Slavoj Žižek characterizes as the "injunction to enjoy," namely, the idea that we fail to lead fulfilling lives unless we manage to devour the various fruits of our advanced consumer culture. That is, we are driven to look for satisfaction and excitement from the countless products that flash across our television screens on a nightly basis. We become convinced that wearing the right perfume, the correct shade of lipstick, the perfect pair of cuff links, the prestigious label of shirts, the high-powered tie, or the adorable handbag we bought on sale will give us some of the zest we are looking for. The commercial offerings of our world are in fact so abundant that we can at times feel slightly overwhelmed by them, with the result that we spend precious hours, days, and weeks of our time looking for just the right products. What is more, because there are countless sleek and shiny things to entice our attention, and thus countless invitations to gluttony, we sometimes become desperate to find ways to control our consumption. We go on strict diets and—to borrow some of Žižek's examples—drink coffee without caffeine, eat sweets without sugar, smoke cigarettes without nicotine, and gulp beer without alcohol. Often enough, we end up alternating between overstimulation and exhaustion so that, in the evening, we take sleeping pills to calm ourselves down, and in the morning, we purchase a double latté to nudge ourselves awake.

On the other hand, we are taught to believe that having deep passions is foolish at best and dangerous at worst. We live in a cultural moment that is suspicious of ardent desires and strong commitments, propagating the idea that few things in life matter, that we have outlived ideals and ethical principles, and that comprehensive cultural change is impossible. Many of us have adopted the view that because we cannot remedy the enormous inequalities of the social world, we should not even bother to try. We have resigned ourselves to the idea that in the long haul nothing we do has any real impact and that caring too much is consequently a waste of our energies. By the same token, our (postmodern and sophisticated) recognition that meaning is inherently relative at times causes us to stop looking for meaning altogether. Though we are surrounded by a multitude of objects, artifacts, cultural icons, and shimmering images, few of these items manage to affect us on a deep level. In some ways, we are increasingly reconciled to the idea that the best we can do is to avoid the more crushing disillusionments of life—that the less we invest ourselves, the more inoculated we are against the misfortunes of the world.

Beyond Romantic Nihilism

When it comes to romantic love, this nihilistic attitude leads to the conviction that lovers are more or less replaceable. Popular self-help treatises are, these days, full of advice on how to engage in casual affairs without getting hurt, how to stay emotionally detached so as to stay in control, how to manipulate our lovers by withholding sex or affection, how to play the marriage game so that we end up with a ring on our finger, how to learn to read the (more or less superficial) signs of commitment correctly, how to jumpstart a flagging relationship by making ourselves unavailable, and how to bounce back from a breakup by moving on as quickly as we possibly can. Similarly, whenever we experience a heartbreak, well-meaning people around us are likely to tell us that "there are other fish in the sea." We are, as it were, expected to process the pain of losing a person by replacing him or her with another who is somehow supposed to be equivalent or even superior.

The intuition behind such advice is correct in the sense that by far the most effective way to overcome an old passion is to find a new, equally engaging one: it is to the degree that we become absorbed in a fresh emotional reality that we are able to surmount (and sometimes even to forget) the past. However, what this advice overlooks is that some of our love losses by definition demand a lengthy period of mourning; it ignores the fact that the kind of love that touches the "truth" of our being calls for a high level of dedication—that we cannot really be in love without being fully invested. This is why I think that those self-help approaches that focus on the right "strategies" for securing our romantic success are more than a little bizarre. Such approaches are usually so keen to teach us how to trick our partner into giving us what we want that they deem any sign of relational devotion—of the kind of unqualified loyalty that prompts us to act without consideration of costs and benefits—as a failure to follow the "plan" correctly. That is, they contribute to our culture's increasing emotional anemia by painting any great passion, any acute romantic entanglement, as an ill-advised and reckless nose-dive into the shallow end of the pool.

Besides drastically misjudging the character and purpose of love, the problem with such approaches is that the more they endeavor to ensure that we do not get injured, the more they feed precisely the kinds of artificial self-presentations that Winnicott captures by the notion of the false self. Because their ethos is primarily defensive—designed to fend off pain rather than to augment interpersonal honesty—they have very little chance of engaging our true self; they have little chance of steering us into the midst of life. Furthermore, they tend to view any sadness or disappointment that we might experience in the context of romance as a malfunction of our capacity to abide by the rules of the game, particularly the rule of emotional detachment. Because they refuse to see pain as a legitimate part of romance, they try to pretend that we can divest love of the last remnants of irrationality. As a result, rather than speaking to our desire for the more sublime dimensions of romance, they reinforce the idea that the most important part of relationality is to keep ourselves from getting wounded.

Yet, ironically, all the rules of popular psychology cannot protect us from love's wounds. They cannot prevent the breakdowns, contradictions, sudden changes of heart, and acrimonious endings of romance. A more constructive approach, therefore, might be to figure out how to handle the inevitable upheavals of romance without breaking our spirit. A more sincere approach might be to admit that not everyone is replaceable—that there are people in our lives who cannot be exchanged for others without considerable cost. Sometimes we meet a person who, for reasons that may remain enigmatic, resonates on a frequency that we find precious beyond calculation. In such cases, there is no possibility of replacement; we cannot ever find another such person. He is absolutely inimitable and, therefore, beyond the economy of barter and exchange. When we lose this person, we cannot simply go shopping for substitutes.

This of course does not mean that we cannot love again—that we cannot find someone else equally compelling. There may in fact be plenty of other lovers worth pursuing. And there may even be some who are more suited for us than the person we have lost. We may in the long run decide that our loss was for the best. Many of us are able to look back at lost loves with the recognition that we are better off without the person we once mourned with a heart-wrenching intensity. Nonetheless, this does not alter the fact that some of our losses are irredeemable; it does not change the fact that there are times when we need to learn to live with the reality of having lost something that can never be replaced. Much of contemporary popular psychology attempts to deny this state of affairs because most of us do not wish to confront it. Yet the more we resist it, the less we are able to love in ways that meet the needs of the true self.

Passion's Enduring Imprint

Whenever a person feels irreplaceable to us, we love him not because he possesses specific attributes, but because of who he is in the confusing complexity of his being. We may of course appreciate some of his qualities. But our love for him does not depend on these. Rather, we love the whole of him, flaws and imperfections included. We accept him for what he is as an ever-evolving conglomerate of characteristics. Our affection is consequently not shaken by the inevitable mutations that he undergoes during the course of his life. We love him unconditionally, now and always, in ways that elude all rationalizations, and in ways that, miraculously, survive even bouts of anger, frustration, and disappointment. In the words of the contemporary theorist Joan Copjec, "love is what renders the other lovable" so that we love him "as he is, the way he comes." Even if we get hurt, even if we are abandoned or betrayed, we may find it difficult to say that a relationship that made us love in this deep manner was a mistake. We sense, however mutedly, that there was a good reason for our passion. We may never know exactly what this reason is, but we intuit that we have gained something even when we have been devastated.

The imprint of this kind of passion lingers on long after we have lost the person in question. It may in fact never entirely fade. The fact that the relationship does not endure does not in the least alter its power to stir us. Our sense that this specific love, this specific person, forms a part of our destiny does not dissipate even though that destiny turns out to be different from what we had hoped for. To the extent that our lost lover continues to live on within our inner world well after his or her departure, we may even feel that our loss signifies less an obliteration of the relationship than a modification of its form. We can, in effect, maintain a relationship to our lost lover that is as weighty, as important to us, as our original connection. And sometimes our bond with the one we have lost is stronger than the bonds that we subsequently forge with other lovers. We may do our best to move on with our lives and to create space for new loves. Yet a part of us—the most defenseless reaches of our true self—remains engaged in our past passion.

The opposite of this are moments when we realize that our allegiance to a past lover has been built upon erroneous foundations. We may, for instance, have lived years, even decades, in the melancholy shadow cast by the reminiscence of someone we once cherished, only to one day bump into him or her on the street and realize that little of the person we once knew remains. Given that all of us are engaged in the process of becoming that I have described, it is entirely possible for our past lover to grow into someone more or less unrecognizable. Indeed, this process is antithetical to memory's attempts to sustain a reliable recollection of what once was for the simple reason that it makes it impossible for us to keep up with the evolving reality of the person we grieve, over time negating the image we have privately idolized. As a consequence, when we chance upon our ex-lover and realize that he is no longer the same, our emotional imprisonment is suddenly nullified. We finally feel his ghost rise out of our being and permanently evaporate. Such moments can feel liberating. But there may also be a profound sadness to them, for they, so to speak, ask us to mourn the end of our mourning.

Such definitive endings notwithstanding, a person we have truly loved usually wields an influence over us that far exceeds his or her tangible presence in our lives. Insofar as he feels irreplaceable to us, he holds a unique place in the design of our existence. There is, as it were, a peculiar kind of immortality to him in the sense that the slot he holds in our world does not disappear even if he does. Neither the progress of time, nor the practical concerns of our lives, nor the exertions of our rational mind, can erase it. In such cases, we no longer love in "real" time, but rather entertain a mythological conception of a loving connection that transcends the boundaries of actual experience. And we may not even be entirely mistaken in doing so, for it is possible that whenever we cannot surpass a lost love, it is because it carries a vital message about the direction we need to pursue in order to gain a higher existential plane. It may well be that we are not ready to give up this love because it, in some oblique fashion, speaks to aspects of our personality that remain unnecessarily weak or immature. According to this account, if we stubbornly adhere to the memory of a particular individual, it may be because our continued rapport with him will, at some distant horizon, prove indispensable for the development of our emotional topography.

Those we love most ardently leave behind a lasting legacy—an enduring trace that indicates that we will never again be the same. Our inner universe will forever be populated by the spirits of those we have lost. These specters of past loves will remain a faint yet palpable presence that recedes and advances depending on what is taking place on the exterior of our lives. We are dimly aware that they accompany our motions through the world like a silent companion we cannot banish. We may of course try to pretend that they are not there. We may even go for long stretches without giving them more than a passing consideration. Yet when they resurface—prompted perhaps by some trivial incident, a familiar scent, or a detail we perceive from the corner of our eye—they often do so with unmitigated intensity. They take us by surprise and force us to acknowledge that the passion we have sought to suppress lives on within the remote regions of our interiority.

We may create new lives for ourselves, we may make significant contributions to the world, and we may love again (and again). Yet we never really leave our most meaningful passions behind. At random moments, and usually without the slightest warning, they catch up with us, conveying us to a place that has little to do with our ordinary concerns. Such moments represent a bittersweet clash of two different worlds: the one we dwell in and the one we hold within. They mark a nostalgic intersection between our "real" life and a passion that draws us to an alternative and more fiery-colored reality. We understand that we have no choice but to pursue the pathway of our real life. Yet the other life—the one we could have lived, the one we should have lived?—never quite recedes into oblivion. It runs a parallel course to the path we are on, at times disappearing into the background, at other times coming precariously close to where we are traveling.

This parallel life can feel as tangible as our actual life. Because it grazes the most clandestine parts of our being, because it reverberates through the echo chamber of our true self, it can trigger immense feelings of fragility and sorrow. Yet it can also seem so alive, so vibrant and substantial, that we end up feeling that it is here, in this invisible realm, that what most matters to us takes place. We can end up feeling that it is within this elusive "other life"—one that can only be glimpsed periodically and from a safe distance—that we most reliably attain the midst of life. A passion that is powerful enough to bring such a parallel world into existence does not easily yield to the passage to time. Even when we describe it long after we have lost it, it often holds the freshness of a recent recollection. Our memory of it can be so vivid that we feel that we are able to reach back into the past and unfailingly conjure up the outline of what once moved us. It is precisely because this kind of passion is not diluted by time, because it feels ageless and undying, that it can feel like our destiny. And from the standpoint of the true self—the part of the self that asks for inspiration and hungers for the sliver of eternity—this may in fact be an accurate assessment.

[5]

The Edge of Mystery

Throughout this book, I have highlighted the mysterious specificity of desire: the fact that we are frequently drawn to particular lovers for intangible reasons that we cannot rationally comprehend. I have shown that there are times when love causes a torrent of disarray, forcing us to rethink our accustomed manner of living. Other times, it infiltrates our daily routine so gradually that it takes us a while to realize that this routine has been restructured in ways that we would have never been able to anticipate. Often, we have no idea why we are willing to put up with such upheaval. We have no idea why a given person has such power over us. Or why we feel that he or she would be difficult to leave behind or replace. We do not know why the person in question elicits the kind of emotional wakefulness that others do not. Yet we intuitively understand that it would be foolish not to honor the call of that wakefulness.

But romantic love is mysterious for another reason as well, namely, that it asks us to relate to a partner who is not only partially unknown to us, but ultimately *unknowable*. If we think about it for a moment, we will recognize that we cannot even know ourselves fully, that it is one of the main attributes of human interiority to be essentially opaque. Fortunately, when it comes to our own psychology, we are more or less used to this opacity. We know that we may at times do or say things we never thought we would. We know that we may discover attitudes, assumptions, beliefs, and dreams that we did not realize we possess. And we know that we may occasionally startle ourselves by a rapid and unexpected change of sentiment. So, emotional opacity is in principle nothing new to us. Yet when it comes to encountering the opacity of another human being, things can quickly become complicated.

The fact that we cannot know our loved ones in a transparent sense can lead to painful misunderstandings. Needless to say, such misunderstandings are what many of the dramas of romance consist of. For instance, whenever we attempt to reduce the other's opacity by assuming that he or she is just like us, we run the risk of misreading a situation, an action, a statement, or an emotional tone. Likewise, whenever we are too quick to interpret what the other means from our own perspective, we can arrive at a reading that has little to do with what he or she is actually trying to convey. In fact, the other's "unreadability" can sometimes drive us to distraction for the simple reason that we fail to find a way to integrate it into the emotional frameworks and interpersonal paradigms that are familiar to us. On the flip side, we cannot always comprehend why our lover does not immediately understand what we mean. Our statement may seem obvious to us, yet come across as obscure to the other. Over time, we may learn to decode the communicative cues of our lover. And he or she may learn to read, and perhaps even to appreciate, some of our idiosyncrasies. But our interpretative powers are never infallible.

The Enigma of the Other

It is worth emphasizing right away that, generally speaking, the fundamentals of our identity in some ways come into existence in response to the mysterious opacity of others. The French psycho-analyst Jean Laplanche explains that from our earliest childhood, we are surrounded by enigmatic messages from the outside world. We are exposed to inscrutable communications from our caretakers and from other adults who enter our domain. Some of these communications are verbal. But others are nonverbal, having to do with body language, quality of touch, manner of looking, tone of voice, and the overall attitude of those around us. What is so interesting about this is that even when we are not able to decipher the meaning of these communications, we feel compelled to respond to them in one way or another: we know that we are being addressed by messages that await our reply. We consequently spend a great deal of energy attempting to translate them into unambiguous meanings that we can process. We strive, with varying degrees of desperation, to understand what it is that adults want from us. But our exertions are to some extent doomed to falter, not only because of the conceptual gap that separates the adult world from childhood, but also because human communication is, *by definition*, somewhat opaque.

The frustration of not always understanding what others need or want from us is therefore in some ways an inexorable constituent of being human. However, there are degrees of this frustration, and these degrees have a direct impact on who we, over the years, become. I have already explained that human subjectivity is inherently social in the sense that we need the presence of others to attain an identity. Personality, in short, is never something that develops in a vacuum. Rather, the outline of our interpersonal interactions conditions the outline of our psychic lives. When these interactions are too opaque, too inscrutable, they can make us feel helpless; they can cause a degree of anxiety and surplus agitation that becomes a permanent attribute of our interiority. When we cannot accurately read the desires of those who surround us, we may come to feel overwhelmed, even despondent; our characters may become inundated by the persistent residue of our repeated attempts to make sense of the enigmatic messages that besiege us.

One of the easiest ways to understand the power of enigmatic social messages is to think about the aggravation that we often feel in relation to impersonal, bureaucratic structures. Whether it is a question of facing the administrative apparatus of a government agency, filing for permanent residency in a foreign country, or trying to figure out the reason for the holdup at the post office, we are constantly struggling to make sense of the external world. Furthermore, the racial, sexual, gendered, religious, age-related, and other inequalities of our society exasperate the issue so that there are times when we may feel that our ability to correctly read our surroundings is a precondition of our survival. When we are trying to decide whether it is safe to cross a national border, walk in a specific neighborhood, hold hands with our lover in public, or wear a tell-tale symbol of religious affiliation, the stakes of our interpretive acumen can be extremely high. The anxiety we feel during such moments is not the same thing as the anxiety we felt as little children when we could not make out the (verbal or nonverbal) communications of our parents. But it does contain an echo of this primordial anxiety.

The more we fail to decode the enigmatic messages that encircle us, the less secure we feel. The more elusive, the more mystifying, such messages, the more potentially traumatic they are. We can in fact end up living in a constant state of disorienting mental arousal in relation to messages that leave us feeling vulnerable precisely because we cannot convert them into any consistent meaning. In this sense, our perpetual efforts to translate the ambiguities of the social realm into networks of meaning with which we can reason and negotiate can over time deplete our energies. When this happens, we feel beleaguered by the riddles of the outside world without necessarily knowing what the problem is; we feel chronically ill at ease without being able to name the cause of that unease. Sometimes we even become so entangled in enervating webs of alien meaning that we gradually lose track of our own wishes and desires; we become numb to our own needs because we are too intently focused on trying to interpret the needs of others.

Messages That Motivate

The impenetrable messages that originate from others can thus
paralyze us. But there are also circumstances where they have the
opposite effect—as when, for instance, the hard-to-read wishes of a
charismatic mentor motivate us to strive for success or the furtive vulnerability of a friend elicits our compassion. In cases such as these,
the other's enigmatic desire rouses our curiosity in a manner that, far
from exhausting us, draws out what is most noble within us. This is
because such instances of unreadability are coupled with benevolence.
In other words, though our personal relationships may sometimes be
characterized by power imbalances, and though we can certainly feel
impoverished by them in the same way that we can feel diminished
by the larger social world, we do not usually experience those closest to us as potential adversaries. Therefore, we are likely to experience their ambiguities as vitalizing rather than enervating. Instead of
feeling demoralized by these ambiguities, we may feel eager to devise
ever-new ways of rendering them meaningful. And, what is more, our
perseverance is often further inflamed by the impossibility of the task.

When it comes to such interpretative efforts, there is probably
nothing that incites our desire to crack the other's code more than
romantic love. It awakens us to devoted and at times somewhat over-
enthusiastic attentiveness that is prone to intensify in the face of the
beloved's resistance to being known. We of course understand that
we inevitably approach others from a biased and selective viewpoint,
and that we can therefore never accurately capture the other's inner
reality. We understand that we cannot assume that what we think we
know about the other is a faithful representation of who he or she
actually is. And we even understand that the very idea that we could
ever fully know the other is a fairly preposterous assumption. Yet we
are rarely deterred in our efforts to solve the other's mystery. Why?

One reason is that we tend to equate intimacy with knowledge,
believing that the better we understand the other, the deeper our

connection with him. But it might also be the case that we are sometimes motivated to interpret the other's mystery for the simple reason that—as I argued above—we tend to experience whatever is unknown as threatening and anxiety inducing. As the American critic Bruce Fink remarks, whenever we are confronted by the other's enigmatic desire, we are tempted to jump to conclusions about what he wants from us. The impenetrability of his desire can in fact be so unbearable to us that we "prefer to assign it an attribute, any attribute, rather than let it remain an enigma." Even when our interpretation is absolutely mistaken, the act of arriving at a definition that makes sense to us abates our unease. Unfortunately, whenever we do this, we prematurely step into the space of the other's desire, stifling his ability to designate what he wants.

The dynamic I am describing is thorny because there is a continuum between our various interpretative efforts. If we are used to experiencing the external world as a potentially hostile entity—if we are used to constantly looking over our shoulder to ensure our safety—it can be difficult for us to suspend this habit within our intimate relationships. If we have learned that the murkiness of our surroundings can be perilous, we may feel fairly terrorized by the murkiness of those we love. This is something to keep in mind when we confront collective stereotypes about communication, such as the idea that women can get obsessive about interpreting men's every word. If this is (sometimes) true, perhaps it is because women, for culturally specific reasons, find the enigmatic signifiers of our society more traumatizing than many (not all, but many) men do; perhaps it is because women have gotten accustomed to regularly having to watch their step. Likewise, those with abusive personal histories may be driven to interpretative frenzy for the simple reason that they are trying to preempt further abuse; they may equate understanding their partner with the idea that they can keep this partner from hurting them. From this point of view, it may well be that the freedom of not having to worry about what goes on in the minds of our loved ones is, to some extent at least, a result of social or personal privilege.

However, this does not change the fact that when our interpretative efforts impose a confining reading on the other, they become intrinsically ungenerous, and sometimes even violent. For example, to the degree that we associate knowing things with having control over them, our insistence that we "know" the other can serve as a defensive screen against having to confront aspects of his or her being that we find disconcerting. It can act as a way to deny the alarming realization that the other's enigmas can never be definitively resolved. In a sense, we ravage the other's inner complexity so as to minimize our own sense of insecurity. We strive to make the other safely dependable by imposing an imaginary sense of intelligibility on an intrinsically unstable interpersonal dynamic. In fact, the more afraid we are of the volatility of love, the more prone we are to impose a false veneer of certainty, continuity, and permanence on our alliance. Our pursuit of an alliance that we can "count on" can sometimes even cause us to resort to poisonous conjectures and projections that are so inaccurate that they in the long run destroy our relationship.

One way to avoid hounding our lover with excessive demands for clarity is to acknowledge that he is not necessarily any more transparent, any more comprehensible, to himself than he is to us. Even if he were entirely willing to give us the reassuring answers that we are looking for, he might not be able to; he might not be able to produce a coherent account of himself. As Eric Santner notes, the other is impenetrate to us not only because he inhabits a foreign emotional world, but also because he is a bearer of "an enigmatic density of desire" that may be as strange and unintelligible to him as it is to us. In other words, in the same way that I am a mystery to myself, the other is a mystery, a bit of a conundrum, to himself. In the same way that I get agitated—split, torn, or divided—by the tension between my (more or less) composed public persona and my private inner turmoil, the other is caught up in the tension between his various self-incarnations. What the other "wants" from me may therefore be less my rational comprehension than my ability to meet his existential confusion with an open and unflinching attitude.

The other who claims my attention with a passionate kind of intensity—the other who elicits my concern and care—is thus someone who is likely to be as mystified with respect to himself as I am with respect to myself. One reason for this is that, like me, the other partakes in the continuous process of becoming that I have sought to elucidate in this book. He is a living and ever-transforming entity who does not have a fixed identity that I (or even he) could one day learn to interpret correctly. He is a loose nexus of characteristics that evolve in relation to countless outside influences, including his relationship with me. This suggests that the version of the other that I see at any particular moment is a version that I myself have helped bring to life. And it also suggests that, insofar as I wish to respect the radical otherness of the other, I need to reconcile myself to the idea that he possesses an untouchable kernel of interiority that will always remain slightly out of my reach.

The Clearing of Unknowability

When it comes to romantic relationships, the most profound form of "knowing" the other may well be to accept that we will never fully know him or her. By this I do not wish to say that we should not try to understand our lovers. As I have already remarked, we usually possess enough emotional intelligence to be able to arrive at a fairly accurate estimate of what others might be feeling. To insist otherwise is frequently merely a means of sidestepping the exertion required to make sense of the convoluted (or uncomfortable) sentiments of those with whom we interact. That is, the unreadability of others can come to function as a questionable justification for interpersonal lassitude. After all, we rarely require an entirely precise reading of an emotional situation to be able to formulate an adequate response. In many instances, all we need is a decent approximation—an educated guess—that will allow us to meet the other with the requisite degree of empathy, forbearance, or attentiveness.

Yet there is also a lot to be said for the idea that protecting an interval of mystery—a clearing of unknowability, if you will—between self and other is an effective means to sustain a relationship. Again, I do not mean to argue that our efforts to comprehend the other are somehow antithetical to love. Obviously there are deep forms of knowing that only become accessible to us through intimate exchanges. However, love is not the same thing as knowing everything there is to know about our lover. If anything, our coercive attempts to interpret him can over time extinguish our passion for him by reducing the multiplicity of his being to a predictable arrangement of characteristics that, ironically, makes him less interesting to us. Instead of honoring the dignity of our lover's process of becoming, such attempts destroy what is most alive (and hence most engaging) about him. They immobilize him into an inert icon that grows stale from overfamiliarity even as it offers us an illusion of stability.

In addition, when we confuse love with knowledge, we can end up ignoring the less tangible dimensions of togetherness—dimensions that may have more to do with touch, energy, intuition, and unspoken meaning than with verbal communication. Even worse, we can become so engrossed in the task of interpreting the other that we, paradoxically enough, lose our capacity for genuine empathy, for the latter implies the ability to identify with feelings that we might not ourselves experience in a similar situation and that we might therefore not entirely understand. Particularly when we are dealing with a relational rift, it is easy for us to assume that gaining more knowledge about our lover will allow us to repair the situation. And clearly we are right in the sense that an appreciation of our lover's point of view can help us dissolve disagreements. However, whenever our interpretative efforts become a defense against the pandemonium of the other's bewildering emotions, they signify an empathetic failure. For instance, when we are so focused on trying to convince the other of the judiciousness of our reasoning that we forget to respond to his hurt feelings, we lose track of the fact that we do not need to comprehend him in order to be able to empathize with him. We lose track of the fact that we can respect the integrity of the other's sentiments without first translating them into our own vocabulary—that we, in other words, do not need to know *why* he feels this or that way, but merely that he *does*.

Honoring a clearing—a gap, space, or distance—of unknowability between self and other preempts this kind of interpretive violence. It creates an opening between lovers that neither can enter without the other, but that can be shared in ways that augment the lives of both. By bringing each partner in contact with alien affective densities—with unfamiliar frequencies of feeling that radiate from the other—this clearing deepens their respective emotional capacities. It demands each to expand the boundaries of his or her psychic space in order to accommodate the enigmatic stimuli arising from the other. Yet neither is asked to compromise on his or her singularity. Each is allowed to cultivate his or her distinctiveness even as they increasingly grow into each other. Indeed, if one face of transcendence is to reach beyond the self's current state toward an unfamiliar way of being, then the fact that we interact with loved ones who always to some degree remain unknowable to us increases our aptitude for it by compelling us to assimilate emotional energies that are foreign to us. From this perspective, the other's unknowability is less a threat to be subdued than a fount of existential potentiality to be revered.

Luce Irigaray expresses the matter perfectly when she proposes that it is only insofar as we respect the inviolable mystery of the other—that we admit that the other is irreducibly different from us—that we manage to love without trying to possess, control, or dominate the other; it is only insofar as we safeguard the separateness of self and other that we manage to relate in ways that promote the sovereignty of both. "Is it not this unknown which allows us to remain two?" Irigaray asks. "Is it not because I do not know you that I know that you are?" In other words, it is exactly because I cannot fully know my lover that I understand that he exists as an independent and self-governing entity. It is precisely because there exists a clearing of mystery between us that we remain "two" instead of being subsumed into one homogenous unit. In this sense, the integrity of each of us is protected by the fact that we can never definitively close the gap between us.

Irigaray goes on to suggest that the best way to uphold an autonomous sense of identity and self-worth is to defend the singularity of the other. As she states, "What makes me one, and perhaps unique, is the fact that you are and I am not you." My ability to esteem the singularity of the other thus assists the emergence of my own. The fact that I allow the other to remain an individual in his own right—that I respect the unbreachable gulf between him and myself—guarantees that neither of us is consumed by the interests and concerns of the other. The fact that I allow the other to rest in the sanctity of his being, that I resist the temptation to lure him into a cosmos of my own making, ensures that he is never demoted to a denigrated object. And it offers me the opportunity to come to my own as a similarly singular entity.

The clearing of unknowability between self and other therefore facilitates the actualization of both. According to this account, it is important not only to respect the mystery of the other, but also to care for the more reserved and reticent layers of our own personality. As a matter of fact, it is when we choose to smother the riddles of our own interiority in the name of a transparent identity that we end up generating inflexible self-definitions—that we risk becoming boring not only to others but even to ourselves. In this sense, our impulse to know ourselves, or to make ourselves fully known, might sometimes do as much harm as our quest to divest the other of his or her enigmas. Counterintuitively enough, holding back a part of ourselves might under certain circumstances be an intriguing way of offering ourselves to the other. Granted, it might be difficult to tell the difference between a parsimonious plot to manipulate the other through the clichéd decoy of unavailability on the one hand and a sincere effort to protect the privacy of our inner world on the other. Yet there is a difference in that the former strategy can only debilitate the relationship, whereas the latter has the potential to invigorate it, provided a degree of ambiguity is acceptable to both parties involved.

The Softness of Silence

One way to promote the irreducible difference between self and other is to recognize the significance of silence—of those moments when nothing fills the void. We are used to hearing about the importance of communication in relationships, and obviously it is vital. But silence may be equally indispensable for relational aliveness. This is because cultivating a reserve of silence is one of the finest ways of protecting the space of mystery between self and other. Forms of communication that are interwoven with silence are breezier, less overbearing, than those that are driven by an urgent need to verbalize every movement of our interiority. The latter can overwhelm our lover by leaving no space for him or her to speak from. Our words can become so all-encompassing and encroaching that they close the clearing that makes relating possible in the first place. In contrast, the softness of silence may enable us to remain more genuinely attentive to the other. It may allow the relationship to develop in directions that constant communication might impede.

I am by no means arguing that there should be no communication between lovers. And I am aware that silence can be used aggressively, or more specifically, passive-aggressively, as a way to resist being pulled into an intersubjective exchange that we would prefer to avoid. I am merely pointing out that communication tends to work better when it is interspersed with welcoming sanctuaries of silence. Silence enhances our ability to accurately listen to the other's concerns because we are less focused on what we are going to say in return; the fact that we do not feel the need to respond right away means that we are better able to hear what the other is actually saying. In this sense, our silence accommodates the more hesitant of our lover's sentiments. By being silent, we gently receive him into our inner world. We make it known that he may enter this world on his own terms—that he is free to move in and out of our emotional universe without being ambushed, ensnared, obliterated, or disparaged. We convey that we are willing to consider, and to mull over, what he presents, even when it is something difficult to hear.

Silence is a means of containing our desire so as to forge an opening for the other's fragile and flickering desire. There may in fact be situations in which the other feels safe to express himself only to the extent that we are willing to curtail the ardor of our own feelings so as to create room for his inner states and words. If we are too quick to overload the space between him and ourselves with unremitting chatter, we effectively deprive him of the capacity to enter that space. If we crowd him with the insistence of our rejoinders, we make it difficult for him to say anything in return. In this manner, we may startle him into a hasty retreat by a mode of communication that appears to give him no platform to speak from. A considerate silence, in contrast, generates a fertile entryway for what might otherwise not be communicated. It allows us to gain access to aspects of the other's interiority that shut down whenever he feels too rushed or pressured.

Offering a hospitable respite of silence for the other's tentative communications does not mean that we suppress our own needs and desires. And it definitely does not mean that we yield in the face of abusive, insensitive, and inappropriate communications. Creating space for our lover's sentiments does not mean that we brush our own under the rug. I am not talking about a one-sided pattern of relating that accommodates the other's passions or opinions at the expense of our own. Rather, I am talking about the kind of interpersonal dynamic that is able to move fluidly between silence and verbalization—that is able to receive as well as to assert. In such a dynamic, each individual gets to express his or her views while simultaneously embracing those of the other.

In this context, it is also useful to recall that romantic love by definition mobilizes emotional frequencies that resist verbalization and that may appear diluted as soon as they are put into words. This is why we are sometimes reluctant to analyze our most intimate experiences. These possess an unspoken resonance that seems to be compromised in the act of telling. In such cases, we feel that we are able to fashion a silent connection that is more exquisite than what could be expressed in language. If, as I mentioned in the beginning of this book, love can give us the impression that we are speaking for the first time—that we are at long last able to convey something about the deep "truth" of our being—it can also, and sometimes even simultaneously, make us feel that there is no need to speak at all, that, amazingly, we understand and are understood without the obligation to verbalize. Like the caress, such moments transport us to a place beyond symbolization and the intentionalities of rational thought.

The Craving for Solitude

There are of course times when silence does not directly enhance communication, but rather signifies our need to momentarily withdraw from our lover. Even then, however, it does not necessarily imply emotional disengagement. We may, for instance, crave solitude as a way to restore our waning conception of who we are. We may wish to protect our capacity to remain connected to ourselves against the soul-numbing inauthenticity that is sometimes the price of our constant immersion in the norms, demands, and enticements of the social world. Because solitude allows our usual public defenses to disintegrate—because it enables us to drop the various masks that we wield for the purposes of social conformity—it may empower us to experience ourselves on a more immediate (or unmediated) level; it offers us a tiny but delicious morsel of personal distinctiveness in the midst of the myriad pressures of collective life, giving rise to a sense of self-belonging that allows us (fleetingly, at least) to feel "real." According to this view, solitude is a way to tend the needs of the true self.

On our own, we come to rest within the calming confines of our inner experience. In the slow rhythm of solitary moments, we are able to suspend the preoccupations that normally drive our everyday actions and thought processes. As a result, we suddenly have space for the kind of self-reflexivity that helps us better process the challenges of our lives, including the confounding opacity of our relationships. In this sense, solitude renders us more insightful, and hence more able to love, than we would be if we never allowed ourselves to leave the world behind. States of aloneness may, for instance, allow us to focus on relational complexities that we habitually overlook. Facets of relating that we ordinarily suppress may surface to the forefront of our awareness. We may contemplate what we do not usually have time to think about, perhaps even addressing issues that we have neglected in the past. On this account, solitude is less a matter of detaching ourselves from our lover than of cultivating a different relationship with him—one that thrives on distance rather than proximity. It is, potentially at least, a breeding ground for fresh relational possibilities in the sense that when we return from it, we may have something new to contribute; we may have something innovative and interesting to offer.

Solitude can thus be a means of sustaining love and, at times, even of reigniting passion that has lost its luster. Yet many of us are deeply suspicious of our need for it, often reading it as a lapse of affection. Similarly, we tend to experience our lover's hunger for it as intimidating, rarely interpreting it as a strategy for love's recovery. This is in part because it is hard for two individuals to negotiate their different wishes and fears regarding the matter. One partner may construe his lover's desire for periods of separation as a painful rejection and a sure sign that the relationship is falling apart. The other may, in turn, feel depleted by constant closeness, needing intervals of independence to feel capable of intimacy to begin with. Individuals in the latter category may distance themselves more or less automatically whenever they sense that their ability to stay attuned to their lover's needs is declining because of exhaustion or overexposure. They understand that solitude recharges their capacity to meet the demands of relationality. But it is sometimes difficult for their partner to interpret the situation in the same way.

Such discrepancies are an inescapable part of the sharp and serrated edge of mystery that cuts into all romantic relationships, introducing a measure of capriciousness even to the most established of alliances. It may, then, help to remind ourselves that, as disorienting as the other's mystery may be, it also has the power to spur us to the kind of dedicated discernment that we are not necessarily otherwise capable of. In other words, if it arouses our anxiety in the way that I described in the beginning of this chapter, it also arouses our inquisitiveness. It prods us out of our complacency and motivates us to look for signs of devotion so that even the smallest of our lover's gestures comes to seem consequential to us. Such interpretative endeavors do not need to become the coercive efforts to know the other that I have been criticizing, for they do not need to impose a narrow reading on him or her. At their best, they do not seek to stabilize the relationship but merely to respond to its profound mystery. They revere the stirring power of eros by weaving ever more intricate webs of meaning between self and other. Such webs do not imprison either the self or the other, but rather add layers of magnificence to the lives of both. From this viewpoint, the fact that the opacities of love force us to operate within a universe of partial understandings and tenuous inferences is not an obstacle to enduring passion, but instead, in many cases, one of its numerous prerequisites.

[6]

The Ambivalence of Ideals

I have talked about narcissistic fantasies of self-completion, the compulsion to repeat, the life-altering aspects of love, the enduring imprint of passion, as well as the edge of mystery that renders our love lives opaque and to some degree incomprehensible. I would now like to focus on a dimension of romance that has been implicit in everything that I have discussed this far, namely, our tendency to idealize the person we love. This tendency is almost inevitable, at least in the beginning of a new relationship. One might even say that romantic love without a dose of idealization is more or less impossible, for most of us like to think that what we love is precious beyond comparison. It is therefore normal for us to elevate our lover to a dazzling ideal, bestowing upon him or her a variety of refinements, and regarding him or her through the flattering prism of our fantasies. Moreover, there is no doubt that such processes of idealization can add considerable charm to our love lives.

However, as I have pointed out, idealizing the other can be ungenerous in the sense that it does not respect the integrity of his or her self-perception. If we are not careful, our ideals can transform the other into a lifeless object that reflects the specificity of our desire without having anything to do with the reality of his or her being. In placing upon the other embellishments that have no connection to who he is or aspires to become, our ideals can empty him of substance. Even when the other as ideal is so esteemed that he cannot do wrong in our eyes, our ideal suffocates him. This is because we fail to meet his particularity on its own terms. We treat him as an enticing mirage that embodies everything that we (self-servingly) seek in the world, with the result that we erase his distinctive identity.

Perhaps even more disturbing are the times when we hold the other up to an external ideal that he or she cannot possibly meet or even approximate. In such cases, we do injustice to the other by deeming him deficient for the simple reason that he fails to live up to the perfection of our ideal. Because we are excessively devoted to a narrow standard—one that might even predate the relationship in question—we come to be utterly impervious to the multifaceted spectrum of the other's personality, eclipsing its diffuse glow by the entirely artificial brightness of our fantasies. In this way, we actively create a relational dynamic where the other is more or less predestined to disappoint us.

Between Reality and Fantasy

Ideals can therefore be extremely problematic. Yet it might be an oversimplification to assert that they are always and by definition ungenerous. Even though it is important to admit that our ideals can disfigure or denigrate the other, it is also worth noting that the belief that we could relate to him or her in a completely nonidealizing fashion is founded on the somewhat dubious assumption that we can easily tell the difference between the "reality" of the other's being and our phantasmatic distortions of that reality. The opacities of love that I discussed in the previous chapter already blur the line between "reality" and "fantasy." But our capacity to distinguish between the two might be compromised on an even more fundamental level.

Ever since the Enlightenment, Western culture has advocated the idea that science, reason, and our logical capacities empower us to relate to the world objectively, as "it really is." According to this view, rationality frees us from the fantasies, illusions, mystifications, and superstitions of earlier worldviews. It represents an advancement over the narrow-minded and oppressive prejudices of premodern societies. And it dissolves imaginary webs of fancy that threaten to confuse our eagle-eyed perception of reality.

The advantages of this perspective are indisputable. However, recent developments in philosophy and science alike have called into question the principles of scientific objectivity, highlighting the ways in which our claims about the world (as well as about ourselves) always necessarily reflect the value systems within which we operate. More specifically, we now know that many of the things we assume to be commonsensical are merely social conventions that have become so thoroughly ingrained in our psyches that we have lost track of their conventional status and come to regard them as unquestionably true. As Nietzsche alleges, "Truths are illusions which we have forgotten are illusions; they are metaphors that have become worn out and have been drained of sensuous force, coins which have lost their embossing and are now considered as metal and no longer as coins."

This way of looking at things reveals that truths are metaphors that have over time become so familiar to us that we no longer recognize them as such, but rather take them to express "reality" in its pure and unadulterated form. That is, more or less every "truth" of ours was once a metaphor: a representation (a symbol, a simile, a fiction, a fable, etc.) invented by the human mind. By this I do not mean to say that there exists no reality independently of human representations. I do not mean to imply that there are no truths in the world, or that we cannot approximate these truths. I am merely positing that many of our most deeply held and taken-for-granted beliefs about the world are habits of thought that arise from centuries of human attempts to sort through it. This implies that all-too-human passions and judgments are by definition woven into their very composition. Since we understand the world only through the conceptual frameworks, labels, and systems of thought that we impose on this world, there is no way for us to know what it might be like outside of our endeavors to understand it. In other words, since our efforts to represent the world influence the manner in which the world appears to us, there is no knowledge about the world that is not from the start shaped by human perceptions; there is no transparent window to the world that would reveal this world in all of its truthful glory.

The fact that the world and its meanings—not to mention our sense of ourselves—are metaphoric does not mean that they somehow lack actuality or that we do not experience them as compelling. Quite the contrary, fictions that have solidified into seemingly incontestable conventions are immensely powerful. As the German philosopher Martin Heidegger observes, our destiny as human beings is to be "thrown" into a world of preexisting meanings—beliefs, opinions, values, and perspectives that originate from past generations—and a large part of our existential task is to learn to make our way in this world. Most of us go about this task in fairly conformist ways. Even though we in principle possess the innovative power to bring new meanings (new metaphors) into existence, and thus to remake the world that we have inherited, much of the time we orient ourselves in relation to the world by internalizing a sizable portion of the time-honored meanings that surround us. As a consequence, fossilized metaphors come to live as integral parts of our private universe, in large measure determining how we go about our lives. Needless to say, this can make it difficult for us to differentiate between "truth" and "fiction," "reality" and "fantasy."

When reality is understood as a human convention rather than an objective fact, fantasy can no longer be thought of as what contaminates reality but must instead be seen as a means of contributing to it. While some of us may be disturbed, and even a bit threatened, by the idea that our beliefs and convictions are merely well-established fantasies, I would say that this can actually be quite liberating. After all, the realization that much of our world has been constructed for us by prior generations implies that we can begin to reconstruct it; we can begin to invent new beliefs and convictions, not to mention more egalitarian social structures. I would in fact argue that the more we embrace the world-shaping power of fantasies, the more appealing the world becomes for us. The more we recognize the ways in which fantasies—and by extension, our imagination—compose what we understand as our "reality," the more we are able to offset the paucities of excessive rationalism.

A rational approach to life helps us negotiate the demands of everyday existence. However, rationality without any input from the imagination can become wearisome and anesthetizing. As the psychoanalyst Hans Loewald postulates, our lives tend to lose their meaningfulness the moment they get filtered through the uncompromising lens of rationalism. More specifically, Loewald posits that the jaded and disillusioned "realism" of the average adult—the ordinary attitude of those who have learned to discipline their imagination so as to gain a more dispassionate view of the world—devitalizes our existence. In the long run, it may even undermine our capacity to conceive new forms of life (new metaphors). In contrast, the innovative individual, according to Loewald, takes care to ensure that "communication and interplay between the world of fantasy and the world of objectivity, between imagination and rationality, remain alive."

Loewald suggests that fantasies can counteract the relentless demands of our mundane obligations. Not only do they provide a momentary relief from such obligations, but, ideally at least, allow us to reach beyond these so that we once again come to see the world as an alluring place. While fantasies might sometimes derail us from the realities of life, they are valuable because they make the world come alive for us in a vibrant fashion. They light up aspects of the world that might otherwise remain concealed, with the consequence that we manage to see grace and beauty in places we might normally overlook. In short, to the extent that fantasies offer us an enriched version of "reality," they render the world more desirable to us. From this point of view, fantasies represent a crucial ingredient of our capacity to enter into the midst of life. They make us receptive to the less utilitarian potentialities of existence by disclosing its emblematic and mythological (as opposed to merely literal and rational) dimensions.

The Generosity of Ideals

The insight that a purely realistic approach to the world may not be the most inspired way to live has important repercussions for our understanding of romantic love. First, if it is the case that fantasies make the world more desirable to us, it might be a mistake to strive to conduct our love lives in an entirely levelheaded fashion; it might be a mistake to deprive ourselves of the world-enriching power of ideals. Second, if it in fact is the case that much of what we classify as our "reality" is a collection of fantasies that have over time congealed into convincing convictions, it becomes somewhat difficult to denounce idealization—and the play of fantasies that idealization entails—as something that robs the other of his or her integrity. It becomes hard to condemn idealization as something that distorts the other's "authentic" personality.

What would this "authentic" personality consist of? How could we ever identify or reach it? Although it is possible to talk about more or less authentic modes of dwelling in the world, it would be difficult to name the coordinates of a given person's "authenticity" in any definitive sense. In the same way that the Winnicottian true self cannot be said to consist of a static set of consistent characteristics, an individual's "authenticity" cannot be aligned with any specific personality traits. In fact, if our identities are always in a process of becoming in the sense that I have described, then "authenticity" could be argued to be nothing more than our capacity to undertake this process with a degree of adventurousness. In the same way that the true self does not connote an essential core of individuality but merely expresses a person's aptitude for creative living, "authenticity" consists of a mixture of spirit, imagination, audacity, and courage. But this does not get us very far in being able to tell ideals apart from reality.

We are used to thinking that love is only legitimate when it is divested of ideals—when we are able to consider our beloved objectively, outside the intoxicating trappings of illusion. We also tend to believe that even if we initially allow ourselves to be misled by the delusions of our overactive imagination, we will eventually be able to banish such delusions so as to get to know the other in a more realistic fashion. However, as soon as we recognize that an idealized version of the other is not necessarily any less "authentic" (or "accurate") than any other version, we are asked to consider the possibility that idealization is simply a particularly indulgent manner of relating to him. As soon as we admit that idealization is merely one way, among others, of interpreting the other, we are invited to acknowledge that it is in fact a remarkably charitable means of illuminating what is most enchanting about the other.

How we see a person depends on what we look for, and therefore, ultimately, on who we are. What we cherish or reject in the other reflects our values, character, personal history, and hopes for the future. Some of us approach others with undemanding and straightforward generosity, focusing on features that are engaging, agreeable, or striking in the positive sense of the term. Others observe people with a degree of cold and critical detachment, choosing to perceive primarily what is defective or blemished. Against this backdrop, an adamant refusal to idealize might indicate not only a lack of kindness, but also a dearth of imagination. It might represent a somewhat insincere attempt to deny the fact that love gains its momentum from the elevation of an ordinary person into the dignity of someone extraordinary. After all, what sets the one we love apart from others is exactly the fact that he or she is not prosaic in our eyes. The beloved is, by definition, someone special—someone who inspires us because he connects us to the more lyrical aspects of life. We are enthralled in part precisely because he introduces a dash of otherworldly splendor to our existence.

The idea that we should meet the other in strictly nonidealizing ways thus devalues him in the sense that it replaces a lofty image of him as extraordinary by a less tolerant vision of him as uncompromisingly ordinary. Even though we are taught to think that we can elude the falsifications of fantasy by taking a pragmatic approach to our love lives, our conception of our lover as ordinary is in some ways no less drastic an infringement of his integrity than our fantasy of his extraordinariness. After all, if we can never know the other "as he really is," why should we not highlight those aspects of him that thrill our imagination? Indeed, given that we can only approach the other obliquely, through a trellis of gestures and communications that offer us indirect glimpses of his ever-receding interiority, idealizations could be said to be well-meaning interpretations that we place on these glimpses in order to constitute a workable map of an actuality that we cannot entirely grasp. Idealizations, in sum, are a lenient means of drawing inferences in situations where we do not hold any hard facts.

Ideals That Deplete

Does this give us license to read the other in whichever way we please? Definitely not. The recognition that a down-to-earth approach to the other is not necessarily any more accurate than one based on idealizations should not be taken to mean that all forms of idealization are equally valid or ethically defensible. There are idealizations that are violating in the sense that I outlined in the beginning of this chapter because they rely on external criteria of attractiveness, measuring the other against a standard that is intrinsically foreign to him and that consequently makes him feel inadequate or defective. More generous idealizations, in contrast, manage to release marginalized dimensions of the other's being, lovingly animating characteristics that do actually exist but that might ordinarily be muted. They might, for instance, play up an exquisite feature that has been neglected or undervalued in the past. In this way, they allow understated aspects of the other's personality to sparkle and shine.

There are thus more or less productive, more or less benevolent, ways to idealize. There is an enormous difference between idealizations that are ignited by some (visible or invisible) detail of the other's being that we find riveting, and ones that arise solely from our own narcissistic preferences. An adoring amplification of attributes that the other possesses—and enjoys possessing—is much less damaging than worshipping qualities that do not in the least correspond to how he views himself. As the psychoanalyst Stephen Mitchell aptly asserts, whether the idealizations of love are enriching or depleting "depends on the way they are positioned in relation to actuality." "Do they encourage an episodic selectivity and elaboration of the beauty of the partner?" Mitchell asks. "Or do they foster the illusion that there are other potential partners in the world who are only beautiful and never disappointing?" If the latter, they have no chance of making a positive contribution to our love lives.

Furthermore, even with idealizations that reflect the other's self-image, it is vital to allow ample room for disappointment. An expectation of consistency—an expectation that the other will unfailingly meet our ideal—is disastrous in depriving him of the capacity to be less than perfect. A relational dynamic that does not tolerate the occasional crumbling of ideals cannot but be insufferably tyrannical, for it effectively shuts down the other's aptitude for spontaneous self-expression. Whenever the other senses that his ability to meet our ideal is a precondition of our love, idealization ceases to be a gift of affection and becomes, rather, an insidious tool of blackmail whereby we strip the other of the right to show himself fallible. In this sense, idealization can be compatible with love only when it is clear to both parties that the relationship will survive the collapse of ideals.

We cannot, then, afford to forget that our idealized image of the other does not capture his entire character—that it is only one very particular way of perceiving him. The moment we equate our ideal with the "truth" of the other's being, we desecrate his status as a creature of open-ended becoming; we immobilize him into an inert notion of what we want him to be. Ideals can consequently be generous only to the extent that we recognize the distinction between the fabrications of our imagination and the lived reality of the other— that we remind ourselves that our ideals do not arise from the other but rather from our attempts to make sense of him. Even though our ideals may not be wholly illusory—even though they may magnify a particular aspect of the other's personality—they are still of our own making. They are still a phantasmatic configuration that, for one reason or another, fascinates us.

The minute we lose sight of the gap between the idealizing gesture (which is ours) and the lived complexity of the other (which is his), we risk sliding from tenderness to terror. We risk turning the magnificence that we bestow upon the other into a rigid archetype that he feels compelled to emulate. This means that, if we are to avoid the violence of ideals, we need to be able to meet the other on multiple levels at once so that our ideals are always merely one piece of the puzzle that comprises his being—a piece that we can safely lose without losing the overall picture. In other words, our ideals cannot consume the totality of the other's reality but must, instead, remain insistently partial. And they must be evanescent enough to allow us to improvise in life-enhancing ways. To express the matter in Winnicottian terms, idealizations that are transient, that are able to lightly touch and accommodate the iridescent play of the other's mobile reality without attempting to arrest that play, are conducive to creative living. In contrast, idealizations that expect the other to fit into a precise (and painstakingly conceived) cast cannot but smother the embers of life.

Keeping Desire Alive

Ideals are therefore neither categorically bad nor invariably good. How they impact our love lives depends on how we employ them, on whether they enhance or enfeeble our lover's sense of himself or herself as someone who is inherently lovable and capable of multiple self-enactments. Ideals only "work" when they take place within a relational dynamic that also—and at the same time—allows the other to thrive beyond them, that communicates to him that he is loved regardless of whether or not he meets our ideals. In such cases, the other is secure in the knowledge that his failure to reflect our ideals does not bring our love to an end—that how we feel about him does not depend on whether or not he lives up to our specific expectations.

Loving idealizations start from, and allow space for, the intricacies and burdens of the other's existential struggle. We know that, like us, the other is an ordinary person with his own problems and insecurities. We admit that he has idiosyncratic habits, beliefs, and patterns of passion that can sometimes be tedious, or even slightly embarrassing. We recognize that he is prone to anxiety, agitation, tension, and worry in the same way that we are. And we accept that there are moments when he can be a bit absurd or ridiculous. Needless to say, he is weighted down by his past in difficult to imagine ways. He suffers from various forms of uncertainty and helplessness. And he defends against pain and disappointment as much as we do, albeit perhaps in ways that we do not entirely understand. Yet we doggedly foster our faith in his ability to glow like a precious gem.

Generous forms of love recognize the other's irreducible humanness. They embrace his ordinariness. Yet they simultaneously remain aware of the myriad ways in which he is also always something other than ordinary—the ways in which he, in certain circumstances, and through a certain lens, becomes breathtakingly extraordinary. That is, while generous modes of relating resist the temptation to trap the other in an inflexible ideal, they do not demean the other by insisting that there is nothing about him that is worth revering. They appreciate the other's regular human qualities, but they do not reduce him to these qualities; they admit that he can also embody transcendent potentialities. They in fact persistently look for opportunities to foreground what is most entrancing about him. At times, they overlook the commonplace in order to bring into better focus what is most scintillating. At other times, they find alluring what others might deem entirely commonplace.

All too often, love fades when idealization yields to the trite realities of a long-term partnership. For many of us, one of the biggest challenges of love is to keep desire alive in the face of the worn routines of life. From this perspective, the trouble with love is less that we idealize too much than that we fail to do so after a certain degree of familiarity has settled into the relationship. The trouble is that, after a while, we cease to see the inspiring qualities of our lover. We transform him into a banal object with no power to rouse our passion. There may even be times when we not only deny the other's ideal attributes but actively seek to turn him into an abject or degraded object. Particularly in the final death throes of love, the ideal frequently becomes its very opposite.

True love—if I may risk such a sentimental expression—must withstand the shattering of ideals, for if we only accept the other as ideal, our "love" remains superficial. Yet, if we only see the other as uncompromisingly ordinary, we deny the fact that he is irreplaceable to us. As a result, we need to be careful that, in our eagerness to build a "realistic" connection, we do not end up sidelining everything that is uniquely luminous about the other. As the Slovenian philosopher Alenka Zupančič claims, the point of true love is not to forgive the other for his weaknesses, or to endure him when we no longer desire him, but rather to conserve a space for the transcendent within the mundane predictability of relating. In other words, one of the best ways to sustain love is to cultivate our capacity to idealize the other even after our familiarity with him has rendered him an ordinary object for us; one of the best ways to feed desire is to nurture our aptitude for idealization within the monotony of everyday life.

True love is not the kind of love that relies on the inaccessibility of the beloved—that generates endless obstacles and preliminaries to the consummation of love so as to ensure that it never becomes a concrete reality. But neither is true love a spruced-up version of friendship and comfortable companionship. As Zupančič points out, true love is not "the sum of desire and friendship, where friendship is supposed to provide a bridge between two awakenings of desire." Rather, it entails the capacity to consider the other as someone who is simultaneously—at one and the same time—ordinary and out of the ordinary, banal (even slightly boring) and inspired (even radiant). Neither the banal nor the inspired dimensions of the other alone sum up his complexity. Instead, it is the dynamic interaction between them that generates this complexity in the first place: what makes the other incomparable is the manner in which the banal and inspired components of his being blend, intersect, and produce effects that make him interesting to us.

Love Beyond Ideals

Ideals concoct a potent mixture of desire and fantasy. What I have sought to express in this book is that one of our main interpersonal and ethical obligations is to make sure that this mixture does not brutalize the other's living reality. This is why it is important that our ideals do not merely reflect the desperation of our narcissistic desires but caress prized details of the other's personality. Along related lines, we need to recognize that whenever we feel tempted to freeze the other into a static ideal that cannot be revised, or that has room for only one version of his or her identity, we may be looking to create a false sense of security in our relationship. We may be using ideals to neutralize unsettling elements of the other's being because we suppose that, by so doing, we manage to stabilize our lives. Rather than allowing the other to direct us to previously unexplored life scenarios—rather than allowing him to touch us in unexpected ways—we hide behind idealizations that appear to guarantee the reliability of our life-worlds.

Static ideals can thus become an impediment to inner renewal: a roundabout means of thwarting our capacity to imagine lives different from the ones we are living. By distancing us from alternative modes of relating, such ideals hold us captive to recurring existential patterns. They may, for example, consistently cause us to pursue relational dynamics that are familiar to us, even when these have proven unsuccessful in the past. Or they may induce us to only court lovers who fit snugly into our preconceived notion of how our lives are meant to unfold. In this sense, they constrict the scope of our existence, limiting the relational options available to us, and depriving us of forms of personal augmentation that can ensue only from a courageous encounter with those who are radically different from us. Whenever our ideals are so stagnant that they exclude relationships that might contest our accustomed understanding of the world as well as what we, as individuals, are all about, we ourselves begin to stagnate. We slow down our evolution because we reject the very lovers who have the most to offer to us for the simple reason that they approach life from a stance that has nothing to do with our ideals.

A love that does not embrace the true (vulnerable) self of both lovers, or that does not tolerate the raw messiness of relating, is a contradiction in terms: it is by definition too stingy, too sterile, and too risk-averse. Even if it is the case that—as I have proposed—there are giving ways to idealize, love must in the final analysis endure the erosion of ideals. It must be able to facilitate the materialization of the beloved's less-than-ideal singularity, including what is breakable, imperfect, inconsistent, or defenseless about him or her. Even as we seek to enhance our passion through loving idealizations, we must never lose track of the dangers of idolization. We must never lose sight of the fact that the kind of love that seeks to possess the other rather than to honor the complexity of his being can only diminish him and, therefore, indirectly, our relationship with him. In this sense, it is only to the extent that we manage to perceive the other as an incomparable creature absorbed in his own relentless and at times confusing process of becoming, rather than merely as someone who either meets or fails to meet our ideals, that we are able to access deeper levels of relational possibility.

The Intrigue of Obstacles

In the previous chapter, we saw that romantic love more or less inevitably entails a degree of idealization. As the nineteenth-century French novelist Stendhal remarks, "in love only the illusion appeals." Stendhal explains that, when it comes to love, we do not easily reconcile ourselves to what is attainable in reality but aspire to rearrange this reality to conform to our desires: we strive to shape reality to accord with our ideals rather than vice versa. Stendhal labels this process "crystallization," describing it as follows:

> Leave a lover with his thoughts for twenty-four hours, and this is what will happen. At the salt mines of Salzburg, they throw a leafless wintry bough into one of the abandoned workings. Two or three months later they haul it out covered with a shining deposit of crystals. The smallest twig, no bigger than a tom-tit's claw, is studded with a galaxy of scintillating diamonds. The original branch is no longer recognizable. What I have called crystallization

is a mental process which draws from everything that happens new proofs of the perfection of the loved one.

Crystallization endows the beloved with every possible perfection. Through it, the object of our desire, no matter how ordinary, is rendered extraordinary. As Stendhal specifies, crystallization implies "a certain fever of the imagination which translates a normally commonplace object into something unrecognizable, and makes it an entity apart."

Stendhal's depiction of crystallization sums up what we have already learned about idealization. However, what most interests us here is that he goes on to suggest that it is the beloved's (apparent or real) unavailability that ensures that crystallization occurs in the first place. It is when the beloved—in Stendhal's case always a woman—appears slightly distant or aloof that the lover is prompted to raise her to the status of the extraordinary. There is thus something about the beloved's reluctance that causes the lover's feelings to deepen into the kind of fixed attitude of adoration that is difficult to reverse later; it is the lover's doubt about the beloved's attainability—as well as about his own desirability—that transforms his sentiments from a mere fleeting fancy to enduring love.

This implies that love thrives on obstacles—that we need barriers, hindrances, and stumbling blocks to our desire in order to fall in love. Stendhal in fact views it a "cardinal error" to yield to a lover's advances too fast because such a premature surrender short-circuits the process of crystallization and prevents the development of permanent passion. As he declares, "We scorn too easy a victory in love, and are never inclined to set much value upon what is there for the taking." Having to work for what we want, having to struggle to attain what we desire, in contrast, ensures that we will prefer our beloved—however flawed or average—to every other available person.

Jumping Hurdles

Female readers will recognize in Stendhal's depiction the advice given to them by grandmothers, women's magazines, and popular psychology alike, namely, that they should play hard to get and, most important, resist the temptation to sleep with a man too quickly because giving him what he wants guarantees that he will merely exploit them sexually rather than fall in love. Such advice reflects the fact that women, in our society, are conventionally taught to be the passive objects of desire rather than desiring agents. They are conditioned to think of themselves as alluring items that men admire and appraise rather than as individuals who have the right to assess the desirability of others. In reality, they of course evaluate as much as men do. But their public role is to be the charming objects of the male gaze. Likewise, they are taught to wait for a man's approach rather than to initiate the game of love. They are encouraged to make themselves ever so faintly available without at the same time appearing too eager. And, most consistently, they are told to "take their time," "make him wait," and "whet his appetite."

As infuriatingly archaic as this advice is, there is undoubtedly a kernel of truth in it in that it recognizes, as Stendhal does, that the idealizing attitude of being "in love"—in the banal sense of the expression—feeds on unattainability. I would say, however, that this is a more or less universal characteristic of desire rather than something specific to masculine ways of relating. Women, as well as men, idealize their lovers, and women, as well as men, can be aroused to admiration by someone who is slightly remote, out of reach, forbidding, or even arrogant. Sadly, many of us—women as much as men—often reject lovers who are emotionally and sexually available to us in favor of ones who are withholding, disloyal, or unkind. At times we even choose lovers who pay little attention to our needs, or who are unwilling to make an effort to build a meaningful relationship, because, on some level, we do not like love to be too easy.

Many of us cannot appreciate a good, or even a splendid, thing when it is put in front of us. We need the thrill of the chase. We like to jump hurdles before tasting the sweetness of victory. Having to exert ourselves to win someone's affections can make that person seem all the more valuable. We may even reason that if he gives in too easily, he may not actually merit our attention. Inasmuch as we are turned on by what we cannot conquer—by what eludes us while simultaneously offering us a hint of all the delectable ways in which we might be fulfilled in the future—we are frequently attracted to self-contained and self-confident people who do not seem to need us in any way. The charisma of self-sufficiency entices us because it makes us feel that we need to prove ourselves worthy of such a person. This person accordingly becomes a challenge—someone we need to actively pursue rather than someone whom fate merely delivers to us. We circle his periphery, longing to gain access to his inner sanctum. And the more he retreats, the more we tend to pursue.

This is how we sometimes become addicted to lovers who reject or devalue us. Whenever we choose to chase people who are remote, we become intrigued—we feel more alive and animated—to the extent that we are refused. And the more uninterested our object remains, the more desperately we seek to win him over. While being entirely discouraged might destroy our capacity to desire, a slight uncertainty about having a hold over our object often inflames our passion. Predictably, such a dynamic does not easily withstand the sudden availability of the object, so that the moment he reveals the full scope of his own desire, we may feel tempted to retreat. We may no longer experience him as an enigmatic source of magnetism. In such cases, our desire has virtually nothing to do with the person in question. The only thing that matters is his unavailability. No wonder, then, that when this unavailability turns to availability, we do not necessarily know what to do with our object.

When Satisfaction Threatens

Is it smart, then, to play hard to get? One can argue the issue in both directions. Those who advocate this strategy believe—as Stendhal does—that once the process of crystallization has taken place and the lover is securely "in love," his love will not be undone when reality begins to consume his illusion, as it inevitably will; the assumption is that the lover's esteem will not waver as a result of the breakdown of his ideal. Others, in contrast, reckon that love "won" through the ruse of aloofness is likely to unravel the moment one makes oneself accessible: a woman who plays hard to get may initially gain what she wants, but she also traps herself in a debilitating dynamic where she is afraid to act freely, reveal her true feelings, or offer her affections lest her availability make her less desirable. She works hard not to reveal "the speck of corruption" that will demolish her lover's idealized vision of her by demoting her to the realm of commonplace objects. In this way, she undermines her capacity to be who she is by consenting to uphold her façade of cool detachment indefinitely.

Yet playing hard to get can be tempting because many of us—men and women alike—have had the experience of alienating a potential lover because of our unguarded enthusiasm. This is difficult to accept because it gives us the impression that our true self is inherently unlovable—that we can only attract a lover by presenting to him or her a version of ourselves that does not accurately reflect the reality of our being. It is, then, helpful to remind ourselves that people who worship inaccessibility may be largely incapable of intimacy. They may be placing insurmountable obstacles to their satisfaction because they, in some fundamental sense, find the immediacy of this satisfaction threatening or even intolerable. They may prefer to desire from a distance because this configuration of desire keeps the object of their affections safely one step removed, making satisfaction more a remote possibility than a tangible reality. And, as distressing as it is to encounter this configuration of desire in our lovers, many of us fall into it at some point in our lives.

This is because, as much as we covet intimacy, its actuality can be terrifying. Loving someone who resists our advances is an effective means of managing our fear. It is a means of deferring intimacy by keeping ourselves wrapped up in a fantasy of imminent satisfaction that promises to make up for our present frustrations but never in the end materializes. Such a pattern of loving can cause us to repeatedly "choose" frustration over satisfaction. It can cause us to obsess about (always unfulfilled) future potentialities to the extent that we find it next to impossible to experience the present as a rewarding emotional space. It can make us ignore possibilities of fulfillment that might in fact be available to us in the here and now. And, perhaps most important, it can keep us from discovering what our life would be like if we ceased to erect impediments on our path to satisfaction.

Sometimes it can be difficult to identify times when we approach love in self-defeating ways. Not only are we never the wholly rational authors of our own emotional experience, but we relate to the diverse layers of our inner lives with varying degrees of self-awareness. As a result, we do not always realize that these layers can work at cross-purposes. We do not always see that even if we consciously believe that intimacy is what we want, we might unconsciously feel compelled to pile obstacle after obstacle against it. This explains why we at times end up looking for happiness through relational strategies that can only bring us suffering. We may even come to experience our yearning for intimacy as the highest form of fulfillment—as what most titillates us—so that any concrete achievement of intimacy pales in comparison; we may become so addicted to the unspoken undercurrents of passion that when passion finally gets spoken, we lose interest in it. In such cases, the attainment of what we desire immediately extinguishes this desire.

The Desire to Desire

Desire is an inherently contradictory concept in that it tends to die or diminish the moment it finds satisfaction. In other words, because we find it difficult to want what we already have, there is something intrinsically impossible about desire. It is a state of deprivation that is motivated by a lack of fulfillment. Consequently, there may be times when we (unconsciously) prefer our desire to remain unfulfilled so as to ensure its continuation. We desire to desire, as it were, rather than to attain the object of our desire. On this view, the "goal" of desire is to generate an endless loop of advance and retreat whereby we repeatedly re-create the preconditions of longing by finding indirect ways of sabotaging our satisfaction. The "goal" of desire, that is, is to perpetuate itself more or less indefinitely by securing its own failure.

This explains why we sometimes experience the aftermath of satisfaction as a gaping void. There are times when this void can be filled by affection, enabling us to remain warmly connected to our partner even in the absence of desire. Our hope in such situations is that eventually desire will rekindle. We trust that if we give desire the "rest" it needs, it will someday return. We may even try to artificially revive it by regulating the frequency of our satisfactions. We may consume pleasure in controlled portions in an attempt to keep ourselves from becoming oversaturated. However, there are other times when, unfortunately for us, the vacuum created by satisfaction is filled by boredom, indifference, restlessness, or even rage and hostility. In such cases, our relationship is in trouble because we have not found an affirmative way of coping with the excess of satiated desire. In extreme cases, we may even be driven to destroy our relationship in order to once again taste the longing that gives rise to ardent desire.

Alternatively, our desire to desire may cause us to renounce a love affair before we have given it any chance at all. We may, for instance, feel passionately about a person but reason that our sentiments are too intense to be sustainable in the real world—that the relationship in question might work in another place or lifetime, but that it is inherently unfeasible under the present (always less than ideal) conditions. As a result, we may choose to abandon it altogether in order to avoid diluting its essence. Other times, we chase a lover from our lives because we are afraid to embrace what we, deep down, know could devastate us in the future. Because we understand that losing an exceptional relationship is more excruciating than losing a mediocre one, we relinquish the very person who could most thoroughly satisfy us. We attempt to control the situation by opting to give up right away what we sense we cannot afford to give up later: we reject so as not be rejected.

These are just some of the ways in which we manage to prolong our desire. We lock a glistening shard of our love in a treasure-box of memories, all the while hoping that one day we might be able to pry the box open again. We cherish the sweet recollection of what almost was—or what might have been—without giving up the pleasant anticipation of what could at some point come to pass. Sometimes we even convince ourselves that the deprivations of love are what true passion consists of. In instances such as these, we can easily fall into a deep pathos of hopelessness and impossibility. We bemoan the tragedy of star-crossed encounters; of passion being recognized too late; of sudden setbacks, endless regrets, and catastrophic missteps; as well as of countless misreadings and missed opportunities. We lament all the heartrending ways in which the timing, pacing, rhythm, or circumstances of our love were ever-so-slightly off, making satisfaction an unattainable goal.

Sometimes, rather than discarding a compelling affair altogether, we try to manage its intensity by keeping it at a distance. We may think about our object a great deal, yet choose to see him or her only rarely and casually. Alternatively, we may string together a sequence of superficial liaisons that are designed to drown out our real passion (the one we experience as "hopeless" and "impossible"): we fill the void of the love that we cannot (allow ourselves) to have by repeatedly entering into short-lived affairs that mean next to nothing to us. Yet, in the end, all of this is hollow in the sense that these other lovers cannot give us the satisfaction we yearn for. They cannot make up for the absence of the one we truly want, even if this absence is something we ourselves have orchestrated. Moreover, the more we struggle to contain our feelings, the more commanding they become so that the slightest contact, the slightest touch, look, gesture, or fleeting facial expression takes on a heightened significance. A mere flicker of a connotation in the eyes of a beloved person we only allow ourselves to see once a year can be more important to us than a full year of intimacy with someone else. Passion, after all, cannot be commanded. It commands *us* regardless of our conscious resolutions.

Sometimes our pathos of hopelessness and impossibility persists even when a deep encounter has already occurred—even when we have already experienced a passion that feels uniquely inspiring to us. In such instances, we disavow what has taken place by retroactively judging it to be unrealistic or destined to disappoint us. All of a sudden, a long-distance affair that earlier felt incomparable is no longer worth pursuing (because it seems untenable). A surprise encounter that just a few days ago felt electrifying no longer merits our emotional investment (because it is bound to fizzle). And an intimate connection that has gradually grown in intensity becomes too dangerous to develop (because it is fated to disintegrate). This reasoning is exceedingly strange in that it turns something that has already happened into something that cannot possibly happen. It chooses to overlook the fact that it is often the clever obstacles that we assemble against our own passion that create the conditions of impossibility to begin with—that when we are more satisfied by the lack of satisfaction than by satisfaction itself, we may unconsciously strive to ensure that our lack, in fact, remains a lack.

Scenarios such as these perpetuate the idea that a genuinely life-altering event between two people is somehow unworkable. But the fact that the event's timing or context appeared inauspicious, or that we did not expect this particular event to materialize, or that we were hoping that a different event would, does not mean that what happened did not happen—for it did. As a matter of fact, the reason the deep encounter, the chance meeting, the blazing passion, or the odd coincidence had such an impact on us is precisely that it was not supposed to happen, yet did. It was not something we anticipated, yet it came about. The fact that the event might have seemed drastically unlikely from the vantage point of the reality that we were living prior to it does not mean that it was inherently impossible: it was merely improbable. And it is exactly *this*—namely, that what our expectations rendered seemingly impossible did actually (at least momentarily) become possible—that gives the event its force. To disavow the event after the fact, and to amass artificial roadblocks to its course, reveals a basic lack of courage.

As the philosopher Alain Badiou asserts, life-changing events are not something we can plan for. They simply just take place. They strike like a lightning from a robin's-egg blue sky, causing, as Badiou puts it, a radical "disorganization in the walk of life." We cannot explain why they happen. We cannot provide any motivations, reasons, or grounds for them. And we certainly cannot undo them after they have occurred. The only thing we can do is to either embrace or renounce them. We can faithfully (and even eagerly) live out the full implications of the event that has shaken our universe. Or can we betray it by pretending that it was not, after all, that meaningful. We can hover in a state of indecision until what happened is no longer happening. We can underplay or make light of it until we manage to make it disappear. When it comes to earth-shattering romantic encounters, we can deem them hopeless and impossible. Or we can admit that, when they make us nervous, it may be because we know that there is something absolutely irreplaceable about them.

The Bedrock of Desire

I have already proposed that there are lovers who stand out from the rest because we experience them as so irreplaceable that even a definitive parting of ways does not entirely banish their imprint. The reason for this is that such lovers touch what I would like to call the "bedrock" of our desire. This bedrock is the deepest kernel of our being, articulating what is most archaic, least socialized (and therefore most idiosyncratic) about us, particularly about our ways of seeking satisfaction in the world. As a consequence, whenever a lover manages to awaken this kernel, he or she almost by definition cuts into unconscious layers of our interiority that are absolutely fundamental to our being yet also a little mysterious—shrouded, as they are, in the impenetrable mists of our prehistory. More specifically, such a lover activates currents of desire that are so essential to our sense of self that we would not recognize ourselves without them.

In chapter 1 I mentioned that although we may, across the span of our lives, meet numerous people who pique our curiosity, there are usually only a few who raise our passion to a feverish pitch. Those who do are the ones who—often unintentionally and without being fully aware of their power—brush against the bedrock of our desire. They stir our desire on such a primary level that we sense that our destiny is inextricably intertwined with theirs. This is how we sometimes come to feel that certain people are "fated" for us—that we do not have a choice but to respect the thrust of our desire even when this desire gets us in trouble.

The famous French psychoanalyst Jacques Lacan explains that whenever this happens, our lover comes to coincide with what Freud already called "the Thing": the unnameable object of desire that we incessantly circle but can never attain. This Thing, in Lacan's rendering, is a fantasy object that we imagine having lost and that we therefore spend our entire lifetimes trying to refind. It connects us to our first objects of desire (usually our parents) so that when we meet its echo in another person, we tend to feel the agitation that Plato linked to the transcendent yearnings of the soul; we tend to feel as if we were in the presence of something unfathomably valuable. Indeed, there is nothing in the world that incites our desire as forcefully as a lover who seems to reincarnate the Thing. However, because the

Thing is a fantasy object rather than something that we once actually had (and then lost), we can never recover it in any decisive sense. We can only ever move toward it in an imaginary way.

Our inchoate sense of having lost the Thing makes us feel that we have been deprived of existential fullness. Arguably, this is precisely what gives rise to the human condition of lack that I talked about earlier in this book. At that point I emphasized that, contrary to what might at first appear, this primordial malaise is productive because it induces us to pursue various forms of secondary satisfaction. Lacan's analysis of the Thing augments this insight by revealing that the trajectory of our pursuit is by no means random but consists of a very specific configuration of passion in that the shape of our desire corresponds to the shape of the loss we infer having endured. It is because the Thing for which we seek substitutes spawns a very particular nexus of fantasies that only a precious few of the objects that we chance upon manage to satisfy or engage us. We are constantly, and sometimes quite compulsively, on a lookout for the exceptional object that, we believe, can make us whole. As a consequence, we fall in love when the object we find appears to fit into, and even to seal, the void within our being; we fall in love when we (unconsciously) sense that we have discovered a little piece of the Thing. In this manner, even when we are unable to identify what it is that we are searching for—even when we cannot explain the "why" of our yearning— the Thing as an unconscious object of longing gives us the treasure map of our desire.

In a sense, our inability to find the Thing underpins our continued capacity to love others. After all, it is to the extent that the Thing remains absent that we are motivated to insert one object after another into the empty slot left by it. We fall in love over and over again, only vaguely aware of the fact that each new lover can merely approximate what we are looking for. However, some lovers come much closer than others to embodying the lost Thing. And the ones who come the closest galvanize the bedrock of our desire, enigmatically conjuring up the Thing for us. When this happens, we may feel that what we desire in the other is something "more" than who he is, that there is, as Lacan puts it, "something beyond all good" about the other that attracts us irresistibly. This something "more" defies classification. It is an ineffable, intangible, indefinable, and incommunicable quality that cannot be equated with the other's personality—that is, as it were, "in excess" of who he or she is as a culturally intelligible entity. It is as if, "within" the other, our desire was pursuing something that the other has come to represent, but that does not entirely correspond with who he or she is. This elusive quality inspires us even as it confounds us.

What is so wonderful about this quality is that it has little to do with cultural conventions of desirability. It should be obvious to anyone living in our society—a society saturated with standard images of airbrushed and idealized beauty—that our desires are frequently almost pathetically conventional. We are conditioned to want what everyone else wants. We value certain physical characteristics because our culture esteems them highly. Certain body parts—hair, eyelashes, breasts, biceps, legs, etc.—become fetishized and carry forms of collective desire. According to this account, we are all to some degree alienated from our desire in the sense that we do not fully "own" it but receive it from the culture around us. This is why certain individuals (movie stars, singers, models, etc.) manage to trigger desire relatively easily and are desired by large numbers of people. We consider such individuals fascinating for the simple reason that they possess an unusually high concentration of culturally attractive traits—the kinds of traits that we have learned to perceive as appealing.

The mysterious bedrock of desire is something more elemental than this. Although certain characteristics of the person we desire may come to symbolize this bedrock, they are never synonymous with it. Rather, it expresses an inscrutable substratum of magnetism that resides somewhere between, beneath, or beyond our lover's definable attributes. It cannot be reduced to the coordinates of what our culture deems desirable but, quite the contrary, tends to reveal itself, intermittently, and in a somewhat baffling manner, through the cracks of our lover's social persona. Perhaps it conveys a slice of his or her true self. Perhaps it has to do with some potentiality or inner intensity that has not been fully actualized. Or perhaps it is related to some unspoken point of deep vulnerability—to what our lover most carefully guards from the probing gaze of the external world. We might never know. Yet we feel uniquely enlivened by it. On those rare occasions when we sense that we have managed to draw close to this substratum, we may feel that our existence finally has a purpose, that we have at long last found what we have spent a lifetime looking for. We may feel that what is in principle inaccessible to us has miraculously become accessible—that we can touch the mystifying kernel of our desire even as it remains veiled.

Love's Apprenticeship

Hitting the bedrock of our desire can be just about the most thrilling thing that could ever happen to us. Indeed, even though our quest for the Thing may cause us to make bewildering romantic choices, these choices are not necessarily erroneous. Our desire for the Thing is not a mistake, even if it is unrealistic—even if the Thing-in-itself will always remain unattainable. In other words, although our pursuit of the Thing is hopeless in the sense that there is no way to refind what we never had in the first place—that there is no way to recover a wholeness we never actually possessed—there is still an accuracy to this pursuit in the sense that it can lead us to lovers with whom we feel a special kind of connection; it can usher us to the arms of partners who meet the needs of our true self much better than the average, run-of-the-mill lover ever could. It is, in short, safe to say that our most momentous loves tend to be ones that bring us within the Thing's aura.

Equally important, the Thing's power to displace socially predictable patterns of desire at times empowers us to find merit in individuals we might otherwise discount. If we frequently fall into routine patterns of perception that determine what we appreciate—and if these patterns make it difficult for us to desire along lines that go against the grain of cultural conditioning—the Thing compels us to assess differently. It causes us to sit up and pay attention so that our habitual ways of determining which people we look at (and therefore conjure into existence) and which we let languish in the shadows (and therefore in irrelevance) suddenly become utterly immaterial. It prompts us to elevate a specific person into the venerated status of worthy-to-be-desired not because he or she meets cultural standards of desirability, but because he or she meets an enigmatic inner standard of ours. This is why our love choices can sometimes be quite surprising—why we often fall for the kinds of lovers we could never have envisioned in the abstract.

This, of course, in no way protects us from pain. If anything, because the reverse of uncommonly strong passion tends to be utter defenselessness, the price we often pay for our most life-shaping alliances is bottomless suffering. Although there is no automatic connection between the bedrock of our desire and pain—and although we sometimes manage to sustain devoted relationships with lovers who animate this bedrock—there is no way around the fact that those who reach us in this deep manner are frequently also the ones who hurt us the most. For example, in cases where we are unable to let go of an unrewarding relationship, it may be because our lover appears to personify our bedrock with unusual accuracy. He or she seems to contain this bedrock, with the result that we find it virtually unbearable to shift our attention to another person even when we, on a rational level, know that we should. Our need for what our lover represents can be so relentless that we are incapable of opening a space for new kinds of emotional possibilities even when it is clear that our alliance undermines us.

An excessive fixation on the bedrock of our desire can cause us to stay with a lover who lacks the capacity for meaningful emotional connection or who may even treat us badly and disrespectfully. We may end up tolerating abusive, demeaning, disparaging, wounding, or mortifying relational scenarios because we are unable to sever our attachment to a lover who seems to epitomize what we most desire. We may even become so entirely caught up in our desire that we allow the rest of our lives to collapse (so that all of our other concerns fall to the sidelines). When we cannot undo the unconscious link that unites our lover with the bedrock of our desire, we may feel that without him or her our lives have no meaning. At times we may even remain obsessively preoccupied long after we have been rejected, long after our lover has told us that we are not wanted.

It would be easy to place a moralistic judgment on this dynamic, and to say that being unable to break an addiction to a past lover or (even worse) to an abusive relationship means that something is wrong with us. However, because we are dealing with the bedrock of our desire—with something that is both unconscious and intensely binding—it is difficult to know exactly what to make of such situations. What is it that our desire is ultimately looking for? Is there a lesson to be learned from being stuck in a hurtful relationship? What might this stuckness be attempting to communicate? Is it maybe gesturing toward dimensions of our being that are undergoing a difficult apprenticeship—one that will at some future point reward us in one way or another? Are we engaged in some secret alchemy of the soul that will eventually convey us to a place of insight? Or are we simply masochistically courting pain?

Such questions usually lack easy answers. But we might as well admit that trying to relinquish a person who incarnates the bedrock of our desire—and who consequently feels irreplaceable to us—can be agonizing. Yet sometimes we need to do exactly this in order to survive. Thankfully, we do not usually experience too many of such losses during our lives. But when we do, we are altered beyond reckoning. Even if we over time manage to get our lives back on track, we will never be the same as we were before this love and its loss. When we surrender a person who represents the bedrock of our desire, we give up a part of ourselves. And we give up the fantasy of ultimate satisfaction; we give up the promise of unconditional love. There is no way to go on with our lives without carrying the melancholy trace of this event into our future. There is no way around the fact that we will always bear (and transmit to others) the deep wound inflicted by it. The wound will fade over time, of course. But it may never heal completely.

[8]

The Initiations of Sadness

Whether or not we feel that the person we have lost is irreplaceable, loss is usually difficult in the context of romance. It is devastating to give up a person we love, even when we recognize that the separation is necessary. The process of reconfiguring our inner world to accommodate the void left by the absent person can be demanding for, ultimately, it forces us to reconceive who we are. We cannot relinquish our investment in an adored person without considerable psychological readjustment. The purpose of this readjustment is to enable us to proceed with our lives without the person we have lost. This is why the initial stages of loss often find us ambivalently split between our need for inner regeneration and our desire to remain faithful to our lost lover. On the one hand, we wish to transcend the past so as to be free to strive into the future. On the other, we may feel slightly guilty about overcoming our loss. We may even feel that to the extent that we endure the loss, we betray the one we have loved.

Our everyday lives facilitate the speedy disappearance of lost loves in the sense that those who are missing cannot always compete

against the intense allure of new impressions, enticements, temp-
tations, and challenges. Since those who are no longer present in
our lives make no urgent demands on our awareness—since they
do not absorb us in any immediate manner—it can be relatively easy
to push them to the outer rim of our consciousness. To the degree
that the future beckons us with multiple invitations to step into the
forward-moving cadence of our lives, those we have left behind gradually whither away in silent resignation. Against this backdrop, our
refusal to surrender the memory of persons we have lost can be a
means of venerating those who have touched us most meaningfully.
Our melancholy ethos of loving recollection can be a way of waging a
battle against the power of the present to cancel out the past.

Most of the time, however, our attachment to lost lovers arises
from the simple (and far less noble) fact that an emotional void is
inherently painful to us. Many of us cannot cope with such a void
without a temporary crutch of some sort: a friend, therapist, work,
travel, Hollywood, alcohol, or drugs, for instance. In the long run,
however, the process of grieving is much more complicated. As
Freud observed in a well-known discussion of mourning and melancholia, one of the most common ways we manage grief is by internalizing characteristics of the person we have lost. That is, we defer
the cold finality of the separation by incorporating treasured aspects
of the lost person into our own psychological makeup; we translate
an external loss into an internal presence so that our lost lover continues to live on within our private world long after we have lost him
or her. In Freud's memorable words, the "shadow of the other" falls
upon us in the sense that the person we have lost becomes an integral part of who we are.

The Aftermath of Loss

I have talked a great deal about the expansion of personality that
takes place when we invite a new lover into our lives. But Freud's
insight about the process of grieving suggests that this expansion

may also result from loss—that mourning may over time contribute to the versatility of our inner lives. This is because we cannot assimilate attributes of the person we have lost into our psychological landscape without redrawing the fundamental sketch of our character; we cannot welcome a lost lover into our psyches without ourselves becoming a slightly different (and hopefully more evolved) version of ourselves. This implies that if our personality always owes a debt to our present lover, it also owes a debt to those we have loved in the past. In some ways, our character is a sedimented depository of our losses: our identity reflects the history of whom (and how) we have lost. If every new loss alters our inner composition just as powerfully as every new love does, then who we are at any given moment is in part at least determined by the kinds of people we have had to renounce.

If this is the case—if it is true that our psyches hold a permanent trace of our past losses—then loss, while obviously a source of sadness, also plays an important role in the ripening of our character. One could even speculate that the more we have lost, the deeper, richer, and more diverse our identities. Though the trauma of loss can initially overwhelm us, in the final analysis it may be the element of life that most distills our being. Each new loss hurls us into unanticipated directions; each new loss inserts nuance to our character. In the same way that pebbles on a sandy beach progressively lose their rough edges to the insistent to and fro of the ocean, the bitter tides of disenchantment polish our personality, resurrecting deposits of poise and dignity that we may have largely lost track of. In this sense, it is in part through agonizing processes of mourning that we arrive at a highly singular sense of who we are.

Insofar as mourning addresses the more mystical side of our being, it may communicate the kind of meaning that is inaccessible by any other means. As philosophers and artists have reported over the centuries, being stuck in sadness may serve as a foundation for deep acumen and inventiveness. Because sadness removes us from our usual concerns, it allows us to withdraw into contemplative moods that resonate with the more reclusive parts of our interiority. It invites us to visit the most isolated corners of our private world so that we can progressively sort through the implications of our suffering. In this manner, we may attain deeply intuitive forms of self-understanding that enable us to reassess our habitual ways of meeting the world. Over time, such reappraisals can lead to genuine changes of direction.

There is thus a potent afterlife to every important loss. How we deal with this afterlife impacts how we end up living our lives. There are undoubtedly times when sadness deflates and impoverishes us. But, ideally, it purifies our spirit. To the extent that it forces us to take a close look at ourselves—that it compels us to confront facets of ourselves that we are estranged from, find difficult to appreciate, or never even knew existed—it asks us to reassess what we have done, how we have chosen to live, and where we are headed; it urges us to release to the world what we most esteem about ourselves. Even if we are at first too injured to appreciate this process of inner refinement, we may over time come to realize that we have obtained something incomparably valuable.

From Sadness to Creativity

It is a testimonial to the tenacity of the human spirit that we routinely find ways to transform love's losses into personal meaning. Yet our culture tends to be so focused on the quest for happiness that we sometimes find it challenging to accept (let alone embrace) the sadder tonalities of existence. In addition, as members of the social world, we are expected to overcome the various setback of our lives as quickly as possible so as to be able to reintegrate ourselves into the productive flow of collective life; we are asked to thrust aside our suffering so that we can, once again, be fully functioning and industrious members of our communities. One of the most valuable effects of love's losses is that they often make it impossible for us to meet such expectations. They force us to sit with our sorrow. They oblige us to slow down and to perceive our lives differently, from the unique vantage point of our deepest regrets and desires.

Let us recall that when we first enter the world, we do not possess much psychological depth. The process of becoming a multifaceted person entails the capacity to digest life experiences that are intended to cultivate our character. Being able to endure moments of sadness is foremost among such experiences, as are the inescapable adversities and calamities that haunt human existence. Such hardships dissolve and wash away what is superfluous about our being, bringing us in contact with the essential building blocks of our personality. Over time, they add layer upon layer of complexity onto our identity, rendering us the many-sided creatures we are. In this sense, the process of crafting a character demands privations as much as moments of fulfillment. It is therefore not always a soothing or a particularly comfortable process. Yet, as human beings, it is all we have.

Suffering could thus be said to have an initiatory value in the sense that a psyche that has not known sadness is not necessarily a fully realized psyche. Sadness, in other words, is not always useless. This does not mean that we should chase sadness, or that all sadness has beneficial consequences. On the contrary, there are forms of sadness that leave us shattered without giving us anything at all in return. And the world is certainly filled with suffering that is entirely futile—that does not lead to anything affirmative. At the same time, it may well be that we cannot reach life's enticing peaks without opening ourselves to its abrupt drops and abysses. As Nietzsche points out in many of his writings, the multiple defeats, errors, blunders, fissures, deprivations, and dead ends of life contribute to the nobility of our character because they almost by definition steer us into a process of inner regeneration. In his words, "You must be ready to burn yourself in your own flame: how could you become new, if you had not first become ashes."

Nietzsche essentially proposes that suffering can over time lead to a nimble resurrection of the spirit. This is because we cannot accurately predict, at any given moment, what we might find valuable in the future. To the degree that the meaning of our experiences unfolds gradually, over the entirety of our lifetimes, we cannot determine ahead of time where we will end up; we cannot know the full significance of any particular event when we are still in the midst of it. Because life tends to develop along meandering lines, our misfortunes may eventually turn out rather well. A sudden tear in the ordinary fabric of our lives may provoke a massive reorganization of our entire life orientation. A breakdown of our usual psychological functioning may lead to an emotional breakthrough that creates the groundwork for a new beginning. Or, we may discover that hitting a limit or an obstacle of some sort leads us to an unanticipated opportunity—one that we would not have stumbled upon had we not reached an impasse.

This implies that it is often best not to pass judgment on the losses of love based on what is readily apparent on the surface—that loss can at times have unexpected benefits. One reason for this is that whenever we experience a loss of any kind, we feel compelled to find surrogates for what we have lost. In much the same way that the primordial loss of the Thing causes us to pursue substitutes, every fresh love loss induces us to try to fill our newly painful void through various forms of creative activity. We may write, paint, compose, take photos, or play a musical instrument. We may figure out how to make a profit on the stock market. Or we may invent new scientific paradigms, bury ourselves in research, look for more effective treatments for a disease, travel the world in search of adventures, or teach what we know to those who are hungry to learn. Some of us become involved in communal or political causes, committing our energies to embettering the world one tiny step at a time. Or, more intimately, we may seek to make a positive contribution in the lives of our friends and relations. It hardly matters how creativity manifests itself, as long as we manage to find a way to invest ourselves in some aspiration that empowers us to reach beyond our loss. In this fashion, loss actively elicits acts of innovation.

Creativity can be an immensely powerful antidote to the loss of love, offering us a constructive means of managing our suffering. When we are unable to mobilize this antidote, we tend to remain trapped in our feelings of remorse and inconsolable deprivation. Conversely, the moment we are able to put some project or ambition in the place of the person we have lost, we once again begin to live our lives. Creativity provides a solid container for our grief, giving a tangible structure to processes of mourning that might otherwise overpower us; it marshals the potentially crushing emotions that crowd our consciousness so that these emotions become available for less desolate use. Or, to put the matter slightly differently, it mutes the sharpness of loss by knitting a protective veil of personally resonant meaning around the raw wounds of absence. Through it, we engage in an alert alchemy of inner metamorphosis that alleviates the ache within our being.

Moving Beyond Melancholia

Creativity allows us to gradually replace past lovers by the countless products of our day-to-day activity. By generating goals and objects that compensate for our loss, it may over time help us transform the void that devours us into a cradle of ingenuity. However, creativity can also provide a more roundabout strategy for coping with loss in the sense that it can, under certain conditions, be a means of prolonging the memory of those we have lost. It can serve as a circuitous method of commemorating those who are absent by capturing their imprint within the meshes of our imaginative undertakings. The French critic Hélène Cixous communicates this perfectly when she depicts the power of writing to recuperate a lost person: "I write and you are not dead. The Other is safe if I write." Writing, according to Cixous, protects and keeps alive the person we mourn, halting, or at the very least postponing, his or her definitive departure from our lives. Writing pours into the abyss generated by the other's disappearance so that the other is reincarnated—venerated and revived—with each new sentence, phrase, idiom, or word. From this perspective, writing is a gesture of faithfulness that is designed to maintain a relationship that might otherwise be lost to the stealthy passage of time. Through writing, the lost person is, so to speak, woven into a text, which implies that he or she will live on as long as the text itself does.

Writing offers a poetic (rather than a literal) dwelling for the one who has vanished. Other forms of creativity may operate differently, yet they all share the power to celebrate the memory of the one who is absent. They in fact imply that absence can at times function as a heightened form of presence in the sense that the one who cannot be forgotten occupies all the more space—signifies all the more fervently—in our psyches; the person who has been lost is, as it were, more present in his absence than he might have been when he was still a part of our lives. Indeed, creative activities do not even necessarily need to be "about" the person in question to be able to render him acutely "present." They can refer to him in faint and entirely implicit ways, yet still hold him in the very forefront of our consciousness.

Although creativity cannot ever redeem our losses in any ultimate sense, it is an exceptionally effective means to mourn. It enables us to detach ourselves from our lost lover little by little, according to our own timetable. It allows us to retain an indirect connection to him while steadily increasing our independence from him. In fact, since no single artifact of our creative efforts can ever provide an entirely satisfactory—or even an adequate—replacement for the person we grieve, loss can animate countless imaginative pursuits, countless attempts to convey meaning; it can give rise to a nearly inexhaustible inclination to bring new things into the world. In this way, it keeps our desire mobile and malleable. It makes it possible for us to sidestep our tendency to resort to rigid commemorative monuments—melancholy edifices—that aim to preserve the past within the present in an unchanging form.

Freud argued that the difference between melancholy fixations and mourning is that mourning eventually comes to an end whereas melancholia never does. We tend to get caught up in melancholia when we lose a person who demands our loyalty so intensely—who is so immensely precious to us—that we find it inconceivable to disavow him or her. The loss of such a person is so unthinkable that we try to pretend that it never actually took place. We refuse to mourn because doing so would require us to admit the irreversibility of our loss. This is how we sometimes entangle ourselves in a melancholy yearning that is at once outdated (belonging to the past) and without hope (unrealizable in the future).

Melancholia tends to fill us with painful memories to such an extent that our desire becomes immobilized. Because it has no viable object, it does not know where to turn. It flounders and our life force drains away with it. Not only are we incapable of pursuing new loves, but our general curiosity about the world may also grind to a halt. Such states can feel terribly heavy. Suspended between a past desire that is no longer sustainable and the gaping void of the future, we go through the motions of life without feeling fully alive. We exist in a hazy state of apathetic nonengagement. Our movements feel like wading through molasses. No matter how much our friends, or others close to us, endeavor to entice us out of our self-imposed isolation, we cannot find anything to desire. We cannot even begin to envision what our new desire would look like. Deep down, we may even be a bit intimidated by the prospect of having to one day name it. We prefer the knowable misery of our past desire to the unknowable demands of new ones.

Against this backdrop, creativity is invaluable because it keeps us from falling into endless melancholia. By allowing us to move forward even when we are terribly injured, it helps us resume forms of mourning that have gotten blocked. In this manner, it shields our psyches from the most chilling and life-arresting devastations of loss. Ideally, it makes it possible for us to slowly transition from the paralyzing space of a fractured emotional alliance to a more elastic form of reminiscence whereby the person we have lost is gently gathered within the pleats of our imaginative efforts. Such efforts empower us to signify our suffering, gradually transforming an unnameable ache into a nameable recollection. They are a means of diffusing loss, of translating it into something that we can endure and live through and, in the long run, perhaps even use as a starting point for alternative ways of attaining fulfillment. From this perspective, it is our capacity to shape loss into creativity that enables us to begin to live again, that (time after time) gives us access to a future; it is our ability to pour our despair into a network of meaning that opens a space for life beyond loss.

We have thus arrived at a paradox of sorts. On the one hand, as I proposed in the beginning of this chapter, being stuck in sadness can lead to valuable life lessons. On the other, my discussion of creativity implies that we cannot fully benefit from these lessons until we are able to enter into a process of mourning that allows us to move past our sadness—that will in fact eventually extinguish it. This is the case because sadness is a torpid psychological state that is, in the final analysis, unable to usher us into the future. Sadness offers us rare forms of wisdom precisely because it immobilizes us in ways that few other life experiences do. But to capitalize on that wisdom, we must ultimately be able to transcend our sadness: we must allow mourning to take its course. More specifically, we must learn to mourn not only the person we have lost, but also those versions of ourselves that thrived within the relational dynamic that we had with that person. We need to grieve not only the person we once held dear, but also who we were in relation to that person.

Giving Up Pain

Mourning requires the capacity to give up pain. This may be more difficult than it sounds, for our attachment to pain can, ironically enough, be absolutely ferocious. Particularly when pain is our only remaining connection to the person we have lost, we may be tempted to harbor it for the simple reason that we do not want to break that final bond. Yet we must in the end find a way to do so, for whenever we resist mourning for too long, we remain imprisoned in outmoded passions. We find it impossible to welcome, and perhaps even to identify, emerging emotional possibilities. According to this account, it is our ability to mourn—or, more properly, to not be intimidated by the prospect of mourning—that makes new forms of life available to us.

In this context, it helps to consider which needs of ours the person we have lost met so that we can start to invest our desire in places that have the potential to satisfy some of the same ones. Even if we cannot ever locate the bedrock of desire that I analyzed in the previous chapter, we may be able to decide what it is that we ultimately want from life, independently of the person we are grieving. What did he or she promise that we hunger for? Is it comfort, consolation, and empathy? Respect and redemption for past grievances? Is it an enhanced sense of freedom and adventure? Prestige, success, security, or confidence? In what ways did we believe that our lover was going to enhance our lives? Once we have figured out the answers to such questions, we can work on fashioning our lives along lines that allow us to achieve some of these things separately of him or her. Even though this may in the long run entail finding another lover, it can also be a matter of learning to attain fulfillment without relying on others.

I have already remarked in passing that by far the most effective way to mourn a lost passion is to discover a new one. When we manage to do this, our desire once again reaches toward an object. We see an opening for novel delights and allegiances. As a consequence, we find it a lot less harrowing to release our hold on former investments. This explains why some of us rush into a new love affair as soon as our old one ends (or shows the slightest sign that it has started its downward slide into oblivion). And this is also why some of us become intensely devoted to professional or practical projects in the aftermath of a heartbreak. When our present reality manages to engage us fully, it is relatively effortless for us to stop thinking about past injuries. We even find it easier to forgive those who have hurt or offended us when we are devoted to something else that fully engrosses our energies. In this sense, it is not the case that we need to forget the past in order to bring about a new future. Rather, it is that we are able to transcend the past only when we become so committed to, so thoroughly excited about, something in the future that our passion crowds out the concerns of the past.

It is important to note, however, that mourning cannot be rushed. In chapter 4 I criticized our culture's inclination to urge us to overcome our losses as quickly as possible. I would now like to add that when we artificially accelerate the pace of our mourning, when we attempt to move forward prematurely, we bypass the lessons that sadness is designed to teach us. After all, the "aim" of mourning is to ensure that, when we are ready to once again pick up the filament of our lives, we do so from a place that is slightly different from—and, with any luck, more astute and self-discerning than—the one where we left things off as a result of our loss. While melancholia fixes us in a groove that does not lead anywhere, that circles the point of loss indefinitely and without exit, mourning is meant to guarantee that we travel the distance between one stage of our lives and the next. In other words, although mourning may slow down the rhythm of our lives to the extent that it looks a lot like the sluggishness of melancholia, its sluggishness—unlike that of melancholia—has a purpose beyond itself. Its end game is to allow us to accumulate the emotional tools that, gradually, empower us to break out of the very sluggishness it insists on; its main ambition is its own eventual undoing.

The Wisdom of the Past

The British psychoanalyst Adam Phillips states with his characteristic incisiveness: "Refusal to mourn is refusal to live. Mourning is the necessary suffering that makes more life possible." Mourning, on this view, is not the antithesis of life but rather its precondition. What is more, mourning allows us to transport what is most valuable about the past into the future. Although there may be components of the past that hold us down and that we, consequently, wish to leave behind, it would be wasteful to advance into the future without the wisdom we have garnered from the past. After all, it is this wisdom that, in so many ways, becomes the cornerstone of our aptitude for "more life." That is, the process of working through that mourning accomplishes is essential for our ability to live well because it ensures that we do not squander the wisdom of the past.

It is common, these days, for popular spiritual and New Age philosophies to assert that we need to live fully in the present—that it is only by embracing the passing moment that we will find the serenity we are looking for. A good example of this is Eckhart Tolle's influential notion of "the power of the now," which paints the ability to cast off the weight of the past as a precondition of enlightenment. This reasoning can be compelling, for it is tempting to think that the less room we give to the past, the less it controls the present. It is logical to assume that the more we manage to ignore the demons of the past, the less powerfully they operate in the now. Yet I would think twice about trying to purchase the present at the expense of the past. While I appreciate the idea that, ultimately, the present is all we have, I fear that the celebration of the now can also potentially lead us astray by, precisely, cheating us out of the wisdom of the past. It can make us forget that humans are inherently historical creatures in that we cannot have a sense of personal identity without having a sense of personal history—that there is, quite simply, no way around the fact that the past is always an integral part of the "now."

Tellingly, Tolle maintains that our self-stories—our attempts to narrativize ourselves and our personal histories—are unhelpful because they bind us to an ego-based understanding of human life that prevents us from transcending the narrow confines of our private reality. They allegedly keep us from reaching a higher plane of consciousness that would allow us to perceive that all of life is cosmically connected. There is a great deal of merit to this argument, not the least because it highlights the spiritual rewards of casting off useless rationalizations in favor of an immediacy of self-experience. However, it completely overlooks the lived reality of those who desperately need narratives of their lives so as to construct a viable conception of who they are and what they might be capable of.

There are a lot of people who have been told all their lives that they do not have the right to a life-narrative. They may have been made to feel that their personal stories were so insignificant, shameful, or inferior that they should not pollute the world by striving to tell them. Their every attempt to claim a voice may have been met with either violence or cold disregard. Alternatively, they may have felt that their stories were being told by others more powerful than them—that their personal histories (and futures) were being aggressively appropriated by those who neither understood their experiences nor had their best interests in mind. They therefore need narratives of their lives so that they can gradually begin to feel that they "own" these lives. And they may also hunger for collective narratives that connect them to a community of others who have been similarly marginalized.

I understand Tolle's reservations about self-stories in the sense that I know that they can sometimes congeal into defensive self-representations that keep us overly dedicated to the past. Tolle is right to call attention to the ways in which we can ensnare ourselves in our narratives so that they start to define who we are, in the long run arresting our ability to participate in the process of becoming. We can even end up retraumatizing ourselves by our incessant regurgitation of past trauma. Yet the alternative strategy of banning narratives gags the very people who most need to break the silence about their suffering. In addition, it is simply not the case that narratives are by definition confining and restricting. After all, our attempts to narrativize our past are always partial, disjointed, and ongoing. Our self-stories are inevitably unstable, and as such, open to revision. Far from offering us a coherent picture of our identities, they tend to showcase the mystifying density of our lives, making it more (rather than less) difficult for us to imagine that our reality could be captured by one story, by one way of slicing the rich material of our personal histories. As a result, they may actually complexify rather than oversimplify our lives; they may allow us to reinvent ourselves over and over again, and always from a slightly different perspective.

Furthermore, although it is true that the narrativization of trauma can sometimes retraumatize us, the refusal to do so can lead to something equally counterproductive, namely, the impossibility of breaking our patterns of pain. This is because narrativization is usually a precondition of being able to work through trauma. Trauma theorists have long recognized that whenever narratives are unavailable (as they frequently are in the aftermath of trauma), trauma remains dissociated, with the consequence that its unspoken energy tends to express itself "literally," in harrowing memory flashes or excruciating psychosomatic symptoms. In contrast, when we manage to narrativize our pain, we gradually transform it into representation. We place language between us and our traumatizing past so as to create a degree of distance from that past. In this sense, narratives—a lot like the creative processes discussed earlier—are an effective means of softening the sharpness of trauma and, therefore, of making it more livable. They are a way of taking an active stance toward what has injured us so that we can gradually lift ourselves out of the position of being a powerless victim.

From this viewpoint, self-narratives are an attempt to ensure that trauma does not destroy us. It would be easy to presume that it does, for there are obviously times when it weakens us—when we find it difficult to bounce back from hardship. Yet, as I have shown in this chapter, we can frequently learn to integrate the traumas of the past into our lives without allowing them to govern the present. Although suffering can debilitate us, it can also increase our existential agility by forcing us to access layers of strength that we might not have realized we had. Over time, our ongoing attempts to process it may even add resilience to our character, making us better able to handle the pressures, paradoxes, and points of tension that characterize human life. In this sense, there is no contradiction between being cognizant of the ways in which past pain is always a part of the present and our ability to step into the now. Rather, the former is the foundation of the latter: it is only insofar as we respect the experiences that have shaped us in the past that we can act wisely in the present.

Though there is a certain freshness to every new instant—though inner experience is sharply new at every moment—the world that we encounter is never immaculate, devoid of the (happy or somber) undertones of the past. And though, as I proposed in chapter 3, we are able to attain fleeting moments of being immediately present to ourselves, the idea that we could (or should) strive to completely shed the burdens of the past will get us nowhere. At best, it renders us dishonest not only with others, but also with ourselves, prompting us to present to the world an artificial self-image that is calculated to cover over our vulnerabilities. At worst, it makes us insensitive to the suffering of those around us, for the more adamantly we deny our own vulnerability, the less empathy we are likely to have for the vulnerabilities of others. In effect, the idea that spiritual salvation is linked to the ability to discard the past can sometimes lead to a strange indifference to the plight of those whose pasts are simply too painful to ignore. It makes it all too easy to judge those who are unable to conquer their hurtful pasts for being caught in an unenlightened "victim mentality." It makes it easy to overlook what those who are more tolerant of human imperfection readily acknowledge, namely, that if a given person's past insists in the present with an immense urgency, it may well be because the energies of that past are too traumatic to be readily consumed or pushed aside.

[9]

The Lessons of Love

I have attempted to illustrate that even when love ends painfully, it often teaches us valuable lessons that we can carry into the future. Foremost among these lessons is the recognition that the outcome of our relationships is not something we can control. Though we can become better at relating, and though we can learn to process relationship conflicts in more constructive ways, we cannot predict how our loves develop. Some relationships resonate with, and provide an opening for, our deepest needs and most dearly held potentialities. Others shut down, impede, or enfeeble both. We cannot know ahead of time which way the chips will fall. And we certainly cannot keep ourselves from being injured by love. No matter how resolutely we defend ourselves against the upheavals and breakdowns of love, we cannot ultimately prevent these from happening. The best we can do is to postpone the inevitable. Or to pretend not to notice it. Yet many of us find it extremely difficult to relinquish our attempts to control the trajectory of love. We find it difficult to respect the destabilizing power of eros. Why?

An obvious reason is that committing ourselves to a relationship means investing a large portion of our energies. Once this investment is made, we cannot take it back without considerable emotional struggle. This is why the process of mourning often takes longer than seems reasonable. But it may also be that we find it hard to give up control because we expect from love what it may be inherently incapable of giving us. We expect security and a sense of continuity from something that is fundamentally erratic and even a bit chaotic. On the one hand, romance feeds on adventure so that, when we first fall in love, we usually do not mind being disoriented. On the other, our long-term strategy is often to discipline our relationships into knowable arrangements that make us feel emotionally protected. We conveniently overlook the fact that passion by definition make us susceptible to suffering. We may even try to anchor our love lives in firm promises that are intended to shield us from disappointment. Yet the more we rely on our anchor, the more helplessly at a loss we feel when it suddenly comes loose.

Before we start berating ourselves for being overly controlling, it is important to note that we may sometimes have a good reason for being a little paranoid. There are times when our attempts to control our relationships do not arise from jealousy or possessiveness, but rather from the genuine difficulties of trying to negotiate the tension between personal freedom and interpersonal responsibility. In other words, our controlling behavior can be a tragically misguided effort to defend ourselves against being mistreated during those times when our partner takes freedom to mean that he or she can do whatever he or she pleases, without giving any thought to our feelings or basic well-being. There may be situations where we are tempted to resort to manipulation or emotional blackmail as a means of counteracting our partner's lack of relational accountability. It is then all the more crucial to recognize that we cannot counter the abuses of freedom with control. We can try to renegotiate the ground rules of our relationship. Or we can leave it. But we cannot force our partner to behave differently. And, in the long run, our efforts to do so can only deplete us.

The Transience of Romance

Culturally speaking, we are taught to value the idea of committed relationships over casual affairs, fleeting flirtations, and short-lived passions. It is not my intention to argue against dedicated alliances, for obviously these have rewards that are not attainable through more transient relationships. And most people in our society seem to want permanence from their loves. Nonetheless, it may be useful to recognize the conflict that exists between stability as a social value on the one hand and eros as an unruly force of passion (and even of madness) on the other. Eros, one might say, has very little to do with the kinds of committed relationships that function as an efficient social glue. Its inherent fickleness and piercing intensity make it antithetical to the task of knitting together a cultural order. We hence make a mistake when we equate eros with secure social arrangements, for it does not easily lend itself to such domestication.

I have already shown that eros can be a profoundly antisocial force. It can lead to states of self-surrender, subvert the parameters of our social identity, and blur the personal boundaries that under normal circumstances distinguish us from the rest of the world. That is, eros by definition challenges the ordinary coordinates of our selfhood. To the extent that it couples transcendence with experiences of self-disintegration, it has the power to compromise our status as self-governing individuals. As the French author Georges Bataille asserts, the purpose of eros is to bring about a temporary annihilation of the structures that guide social behavior. He in fact specifies that the transition from everyday sociality to erotic expression presupposes "a partial dissolution of the person." The very aim of eros, then, is to unravel the individual as a social entity.

This insight invites us to reconsider how we evaluate the successes and failures of love. If we give up the idea that love is meant to lead to permanent relationships that stabilize our social world, we might judge a brief but sweet love as more "successful" than one that endures but over time ceases to electrify us. We might even end up asking, with Roland Barthes, why it is that we have come to believe that it is "better to *last* than to *burn*." This does not necessarily mean that we should abandon the notion of committed love. Many of us cannot imagine our lives without it. But we might as well acknowledge that no matter how ardently we desire the longevity of love, it is inherently brittle and more often than not transitory. Most of our loves do not last, and perhaps they are not even meant to. To the degree that we are able to accept this, we might be better equipped to lean into the ruptures of romance without getting debilitated.

One reason we tend to find the ruptures of romance so distressing is that we often view them as something unusual rather than as an intrinsic component of love. We tend to assume that love is supposed to succeed even as we are confronted by opposing evidence on a daily basis. Although we, rationally speaking, understand that many of our relationships are unlikely to survive, we tend to enter into each new alliance with the strong belief that it will be the exception to the rule. As a matter of fact, many of us would find it impossible to make an emotional investment without this comforting assumption. Furthermore, we are conditioned to think that the purpose of love is to make us happy so that, when it does not, we tend to feel betrayed by it. Yet it is likely that love's calling is much more expansive and enigmatic than happiness—that moments of unhappiness are as much a part of its native itinerary as are moments of happiness. Unfortunately, the more we hunger for security in our relationships, the less we are able to see this. Our pursuit of stability makes it difficult for us to appreciate the idea that the failures of love might be an elemental (and therefore unavoidable) dimension of its character.

I am of course not proposing that we should enter our relationships with the expectation of their failure. However, it might be helpful to understand that the demise of each relationship is in some ways built into its structure from the very beginning. This demise takes different forms in the sense that some alliances are disrupted prematurely whereas others come to a more timely conclusion. It is probably fortunate that we cannot foretell how a particular relationship will end (in the same way that it is fortunate that we cannot usually foretell our own death), for counting the clock to a specific moment in the future would most likely paralyze us completely. In this sense, it is our lack of knowledge about the future that makes love (and life) possible in the present. Yet we do know that our relationship *will* at some point end (if only with the death of one of the partners) in the same way that everything about human existence eventually comes to a close. This suggests that, in addition to learning to mourn the specific losses we endure, we might also need to learn to mourn the very notion of permanence.

The Mission of Love

Accepting love's inherent transience allows us to better tolerate its ambiguities and disruptions, including its unexpected endings. Consider, for example, the common enough scenario where things fail to work out for no apparent reason—where love dies more or less inexplicably. Our partner may suddenly feel the need for autonomy without being able to offer any kind of a justification for his or her withdrawal. He or she may feel an irresistible urge to escape the relationship even when nothing appears to be wrong. Or he or she may feel cornered even when we grants him or her every possible freedom. In such instances, those who approach relationships with the expectation of permanence may suffer tremendously. They are prone to take their lover's detachment personally, as a sign that they have done something wrong. And they may try frenetically to unearth the motivations that led their lover to desert them, over time fatiguing themselves by spinning story after story, interpretation after interpretation, to account for what has happened.

In contrast, those who forgo the expectation of permanence may be able to let go more graciously. They realize that sometimes love comes to an end without any reason whatsoever, or without either party having done anything wrong—that it is simply in the nature of eros to exhaust itself. They are able to recognize that a lover who flees a relationship is likely to be seeking something that is unavailable to him or her within its confines. This does not necessarily mean that there was something intrinsically wrong about the relationship, but merely that it could ultimately not offer the departing partner what he was looking for. It may even be that he does not consciously know what he wants. He may be obeying a furtive unconscious impulse that goes against his conscious reasoning and aspirations. He may, in other words, be as confused about the reasons for his actions as is the partner he leaves behind.

When we relinquish the expectation of love's permanence, we may be able to let come what comes, and let pass what passes, without asking our partner for explanations and rationalizations. We may be willing to concede that even if a particular situation does not make sense to us, it may have its own internal rationale that we need to revere. As a result, we may be better able to allow our lover to rest within the tangle of his ambivalence. For instance, if he drifts away from us in the way that I described above, we may simply let him leave without a reproach. We may be able to respect his need to do what he feels compelled to do without striving to convince him otherwise. Because we know that we are not interested in love that is not freely given, we do not waste our energies on trying to hold onto a lover who eludes us. No matter how much his departure wounds us, we know that in the end this is a better outcome than one where he sticks around merely because he does not want to disappoint us.

Sometimes the best we can do in a confusing relational scenario is to let it exhaust its momentum without attempting to interfere in its trajectory. Sometimes the most generous gift we can give our lover is the gift of patience in the sense that we are willing to wait for the scenario to unfold without forcing its outcome. We demonstrate our love by being prepared to pull back so as to allow the scenario to disclose its significance organically, according to its own momentum. It is quite possible that we will not end up with the finale we want. But at least we will gain something truthful. We will attain a result that reflects the actuality of our relationship rather than the (ever-seductive yet treacherous) maze of our own wishes. One could even argue that our capacity to allow relational dynamics to reach an honest conclusion may be a sign that we have learned one of the most basic lessons of love: we have managed to give up our attachment to specific outcomes—ones that serve our own needs rather than the broader needs of the alliance.

It is, once again, essential to be precise. I do not mean that our needs are unimportant. Obviously an alliance that does not meet any of them is not worth our effort. I am merely pointing out that the logic of love does not always match the logic of our needs. When love delivers us an outcome (such as a breakup) that we do not want, it is not because it is out to "get" us. Rather, there may be a discrepancy between our wishes and the larger mission that love is aspiring to accomplish. As I have attempted to demonstrate in this book, sometimes the latter has absolutely nothing to do with our conscious wishes. It may even be directly adverse to them, which is precisely why we often struggle so vehemently when we are in love—why love can make us doubt our basic sanity and judgment. Yet the more we struggle, the more difficult we make it for love to complete its assignment (unless, of course, this assignment is to make us struggle). The more we strive to manipulate our romantic destinies, the less open we are to the larger existential lessons that love is meant to teach us.

Undoubtedly, it can be difficult to internalize these lessons, particularly when we do not know, ahead of time, what they are (or what their ultimate objective might be). It can be taxing to allow relationships to play themselves out without stepping in with our interpretations (or our advice, accusations, and admonishments). And the more taut or tense the situation, the more impossible it may seem to award it the space to develop at its own pace, without imposing our reading on it. Our terror of abandonment alone can prompt us to a feverish deductive frenzy for, as I have stressed, we are in many ways programmed to believe that we can control a situation by better understanding its complexities. This, however, is rarely the case in the context of romantic relationships. The fact that we understand what is happening does not necessarily help us steer things into a preferred outcome. If anything, our impulse to overinterpret an interpersonal scenario can make it harder for us to hear our partner's thoughts. In this sense, it is only when we learn to suspend our desire for transparency that we become capable of genuine relationships—that we become capable of embracing the reasoning and points of view of others.

Respecting Love's Rhythm

The more we admit that our exertions to control love are often a hopeless attempt to make it last beyond its intended lifespan, the easier it is for us to allow it to grow or fail to its own rhythm. When we accept that love tends to find its way to specific outcomes regardless of how much we scheme or struggle, we may finally be able to stop scheming and struggling. We may learn to value things the way they are rather than obsess about how we would like them to be. By this I do not mean that we should not try to improve the quality of our love lives for, as my analysis of the repetition compulsion in chapter 2 revealed, there is a lot we can do to dissolve unproductive romantic patterns. I also do not mean that we should become complacent, for love cannot thrive without our sustained vigilance. I am merely saying that when we respect the mysterious undertow of our romantic destinies, we may be better able to discard our energy-consuming efforts to force, change, amend, or stage-manage situations that reside beyond our control. This act of shedding our urge to dictate the results of love, in turn, renders us more receptive to its various forms of aliveness; it enables us to welcome love's unexpected twists and turns as sites of newly rising opportunities.

Giving up control does not imply a lack of emotional investment. It does not prevent us from forming an intimate and profound connection to the one we love. The very opposite may in fact be the case in the sense that an awareness of the frailties of love may keep our relationship from solidifying into a tiresome routine. When we know that things may not always remain the same—when we expect the unexpected, as it were—we are much more likely to pay attention to the details of what we are doing; we are more likely to remain self-aware and keenly observant. From this viewpoint, our task is to tend our love with sensitivity, dedication, and thoughtfulness while at the same time doing our best to fend off the fear of impermanence, for this fear can make us overly tentative and unspontaneous. It can introduce a deadly kind of guardedness to our alliance that over time robs it of its vitality. Indeed, one of the ironies of love is that our efforts to render it secure can stifle the very spirit of exploration and improvisation that captivated us in the first place.

We tend to think of passion as something that materializes more or less unprompted. However, there are clearly circumstances that are more conducive to it than others. Even if it initially emerges without being intentionally elicited, in the long run it needs to be cared for. A fluid relational dynamic that is able to accommodate the unexpected is much better designed to promote passion than one that assumes that the future is known in advance. For one thing, such a dynamic makes us receptive to the unique integrity of each moments as it unfolds. We come to appreciate each moment for what that moment can yield because we understand that we might never be able to replicate it. On this account, our awareness of love's transience increases, rather than diminishes, its worth. Rather that viewing the decay or fading away of love as a defect of existence, we understand that love's fleeting character only enhances its preciousness. In this fashion, our readiness to accept the likelihood that our love will come to an end, paradoxically, makes it possible for us to fully enjoy it while we still have it.

Life without turmoil—and love without ruptures—is difficult to achieve. Human beings are not intended for unperturbed lives in the sense that abrupt tears in the texture of our existence are inescapable. However, this is not necessarily a bad thing, for if the status quo of our lives was not once in a while shaken to the core, we might never discover the existential potentialities that remain obscured by our habitual manner of going about our activities. There may well be times when a destabilizing rupture is what we need in order to wake up and properly see what in our lives needs to be reevaluated. That is, even if love's ruptures initially cause us to become fixated on the details of our despair—particularly on how, where, and why we went wrong—they can in due course prod us out of our complacency into a new kind of responsibility to ourselves. They can alert us to the ways in which we feel thwarted, blocked, or dissatisfied in our lives, thereby summoning us to become active participants in the molding of our futures.

The Fidelity to Love

Inner growth happens in spurts rather than in an even-keeled and foreseeable manner. Moments when things do not work out for us, when our best laid plans are derailed, are often rife with opportunity. I would consequently say that our fidelity (our uncompromising faithfulness) to love means not only that we honor the particular pact that we have made with our lover, but also that we recognize that no matter what happens, our life has been radically and irreversibly altered. It means that we are being asked to reinterpret our entire existence from the perspective of our love. This is what Alain Badiou has in mind when he writes, "Under the effect of a loving encounter, if I want to be really faithful to it, I must completely rework my ordinary way of living." According to Badiou, love is a life-altering event precisely to the extent that it represents a radical "break" in the normal order of our existence. We simply cannot carry on as if nothing had happened but are compelled to invent new modes of going about our preoccupations. Love is a matter of being-two, or of being-together, that exceeds our own private being and that, therefore, demands that we reconceive who we are. It asks us to measure ourselves against something that is beyond us yet so close to us that we cannot easily disentangle ourselves from it.

There may be times when it is tempting to betray this process—when we would rather walk away (or settle for a mediocre relationship) than keep trying to reconfigure our whole way of being. And the longer a relationship endures, the more challenging it may become for us to persist in the task, for our willingness to do so tends to erode with the attrition of ardor. Yet if we wish to remain faithful to love's summons, we must allow it to keep changing us. It may even be possible to tell the difference between a prosaic love affair and an authentic passion by assessing its overall impact on our lives. If we are able to continue living as we always have, our encounter may not be terribly profound. But if we are repeatedly forced to rethink our path, we may have come across a life-defining force that will in the long run give rise to a new destiny. One way to stay faithful to love is to remain alive to this force, no matter how strange or disruptive it appears.

I do not wish here to imply that we should stay in a problematic relationship merely for the sake of some abstract notion of faithfulness. Sometimes the best we can do is to leave a relationship that has lost its charm (or that is hurting us). In such cases, the courage to walk away may be a much more robust display of fidelity than the decision to stay at the cost of our joy or welfare. In other words, I am by no means suggesting that all love affairs merit our fidelity. I am simply proposing that when we respect love as an event that has the power to decenter us, we may be better able to resist the inclination to retreat at the first sign of trouble. We may be willing to reformulate love's parameters over and over again in order to keep ourselves from falling into a rigid idea of what it should be like. We may be willing to work through frictions until we reach a more positive platform to stand on. And we may be willing to endure some discomfort, and perhaps even to sacrifice some of our own interests, in order to carve a trail to the far side of relational dilemmas. Again, this is not a matter of forfeiting our dignity or self-respect. But our ability to question the musty (and at times quite obstinate) conventions that govern our existence may allow us to meet the more tempestuous layers of love with a measure of adroitness.

This kind of fidelity ensures that a relationship is able to endure considerable stress without being irreversibly damaged—that it has space for moments of wavering and hesitancy along with heartfelt affection. This is because both partners in such an alliance refrain from interpreting their occasional bouts of dissonance as the end of their love, regarding them instead as temporary pauses in its expression. They patiently wait for love to reemerge from such pauses without attempting to artificially rush its step. This may be unnerving at times. Yet, strangely enough, lovers who are devoted to this type of fidelity can count on each other even amidst major relational instability, for they know that the latter cannot ultimately disband their loyalty to their love. It cannot extinguish their dedication to the give and take of relating, or their determination to cope, in good faith, with whatever comes their way.

One of the most demanding things about fidelity of this kind is that it frequently asks us to act without knowing the true character of a given situation. It obliges us to make important decisions on the basis of imprecise intuitions, conjectures, hypotheses, and probabilities, with the result that we cannot even begin to prophesy their outcome. All we know is that if we wait for certainty, if we wait until conditions are perfect, we are likely to miss our window of opportunity. We take a chance because we understand that waiting for external circumstances to click into place will arrest the momentum of the situation. If we make the wrong decision, we may inadvertently trap ourselves in a negative dynamic. But often enough, we are later able to look back at our action and to relish the knowledge that it is only because we had the nerve to proceed based on imperfect information that wonderful things came about; we know that our capacity to make a decision without being certain of its consequences gave us something worthwhile.

Love as a Process

Love is a series of hopes and wishes, small defeats and large losses. It may then be that our fidelity to love is, in the final analysis, a matter of staying dedicated to love *as a process*. If our relationships are characterized by chance events, accidents, and contingencies, the blissful highs of rapture and the bitter lows of discontent, as well as moments when, seemingly without any cause, desire comes to a full stop, then the only way to remain loyal to it is to let it run its course without worrying too much about how things will turn out in the end. Indeed, accepting that our loves are likely to remain partially opaque and a bit bewildering frees us to delve into their uncertainties without any expectation that we will ever fully neutralize these uncertainties. It allows us to remain fiercely attentive to the here and now of our love, while at the same time staying mindful of the myriad shifts that by necessity always crowd the horizon.

Fidelity of this kind is in some ways the very antithesis of a static commitment. It is a devotion to the process of love in the face of considerable ambivalence rather than an attempt to preserve the established traditions of a relationship. The two lovers involved in such fidelity are less interested in shielding their relationship from change than in what they can, over time, and in an always imperfect manner, build *between* themselves—in how their love allows them to continually reach beyond their personal limitations. The evolving space between them—a space that is not the property of either but belongs to both of them equally—is saturated with currents of energy that vitalize both. They observe the mutations of this energy with genuine fascination. And they draw on it to assemble a future that accommodates both without constraining either. This energy is in principle a bottomless spring of mutual expansion, provided both partners remain committed to tending it.

Our inclination to abandon our fidelity to a process of this kind is perhaps the greatest when love lets us down, and particularly when we are confronted by one of its cynical and distrustful endings. As I have already observed, it can be tempting to interpret a failed love affair as something that was never very important to begin with (even if it once meant everything to us). We can retroactively lose faith in the choices we made, convincing ourselves that what we thought was a genuine passion was a terrible lapse of discrimination, and blaming ourselves for allowed ourselves to be so piteously hoodwinked. In such situations, when we look back, we detect only a humiliating misstep. Alternatively, our disillusionment can induce us to a caustic renunciation of the entire affair, so that we lose sight of all the reasons for which we formerly enjoyed it. We find fault everywhere, no longer able to perceive a complicated relational tapestry that contains not only what has injured us, but also past delights and pleasures. In this way, we betray not only the love we once felt, but also our previous judgment.

When love ends painfully, it is easy to condemn ourselves for having been foolish or imprudent. However, what I have tried to show in this book is that such a verdict may result from a shallow appraisal of what love is supposed to accomplish. I have sought to reveal that the aim of love may be less to make us satisfied or comfortable than to initiate us to nuances of human experience that might otherwise elude us. From this perspective, there are few mistakes in love. There are no mishaps, but merely fresh opportunities for learning. Even the worst of love's disappointments can, over time, yield things of consequence.

When we think of other aspects of life, we usually have no trouble understanding this. We recognize that the fact that some of our actions turn out to be erroneous does not mean that we cannot garner some nugget of wisdom from them. By the same token, it may be possible to interpret the "errors" of love as potential insights, and to resolve to give them the necessary time and space to mature into emotional intelligence. There is of course no guarantee that we will ever reap the benefits of such intelligence. But our chances of doing so are greater if we choose to read the ruptures of love as latent openings to previously unexplored forms of self-experience.

Each of us is made up of many lives in the sense that we are composed of countless existential possibilities. Yet, at any given time, we are able to pursue only one of these lives. Perhaps, then, it is the case that what we experience as a debilitating mistake is merely one of our "other" lives erupting to the surface. Perhaps we are being asked to live a life that we never knew was within us. This life is not necessarily any better or worse than the other possible lives we could be living. It is merely different. Yet the fact that we are being invited to live it implies that there is potentially something of value in it for us. If the failures and malfunctions of passion disorient us, perhaps we are being urged to follow the thread of that disorientation; perhaps we are being exhorted to assess our lives against new kinds of criteria. On this view, our fidelity to love includes our willingness to enter into a process of elaborating the meaning of even its most traumatic disenchantments.

How we see the matter depends, once again, on how we envision the function of pain in human life. There are those who believe that the best thing to do with traumatic events—including the failures and malfunctions of passion—is to leave them behind as swiftly as possible. From their standpoint, not being able to conquer the distressing legacy of such events displays a pathetic lack of emotional self-sufficiency. In contrast, those who have managed to live through harrowing emotional trials without being irrevocably broken know that it is possible to weave past trauma into the fabric of our lives without letting it restrict us in any way. They know that allowing pain to dwell within our interiority does not necessarily mean that we are weak or unable to embrace the future. Quite the contrary, it can be a sign that we are courageous enough to stay fully alive even during a difficult passage. It reveals that our psyches are capacious enough to be able to contain a rich variety of emotional modalities at once. Indeed, when we manage (with varying degrees of gracefulness) to integrate pain into the singular composition of our inner lives, it finds a place alongside other feelings, becoming merely one aspect of our character—something that is significant yet far from life-defining.

In this fashion, we can make peace with pain so that it enhances, rather than diminishes, our lives. We can come to accept it as an important part of ourselves without mistaking it for something that depicts, let alone commands, who we are or what we, in due course, might become. As I have attempted to articulate in this book, the price we pay for the arrogance of imagining that pain cannot reach us is that it ends up expressing itself in oblique (and largely unconscious) ways that we cannot contain; it wreaks all the more havoc for being ignored or denigrated. When our stoicism interferes with our humanity, we risk developing a wooden emotional life and an equally wooden personality. In contrast, the realization that our ability to work through pain makes us stronger than all of our efforts to exorcize it may in the long run alleviate its burden. It may enable us to take up our destiny as creatures whose very vulnerability renders us capable of inspired and truly awe-inspiring love.

Conclusion

If my discussion of love seems to always return to the past, and particularly to the pain of the past, it is because the object of our love—as Lacan, among others, has argued—is always a "refound" object. In other words, our unconscious blueprints of loving are so powerful that the person we love in the present always in some ways reincarnates the people we have loved in the past. And, as I have shown, our current configurations of desire often revive previous configurations even when we would prefer to do things differently. Unconscious patterns tend to sneak into our relationships with an almost frightening predictability, so that we get wounded—or end up wounding our loved ones—over and over again, and according to scripts that are all too familiar to us. There are in fact few things about romantic love that are as consistent as the always highly idiosyncratic profile of our pain (or of our capacity to inflict pain). We tend to resurrect the traumas of the past with such reliability that we sometimes come to feel that those traumas are what we, ultimately, are made of. One of my main goals in this book has been to demonstrate that this is because the repetition compulsion can be extremely tenacious.

The classically Freudian way to understand the repetition compulsion is to say that we want from our lovers what we once wanted (but could not get) from our parents. Yet the idea that adult romance is merely a rerun of our family romance may be a slightly oversimplistic way of looking at the issue. It may be more accurate to say that if our present desire carries a residue of our past desire, this is a way of resuscitating not just our archaic bond with our first love objects, but our entire interpersonal history. After all, our present desire is likely to contain a trace of *all* of our most important relationships. While this certainly includes our parents, it also includes past lovers and other people who have played a central role in our lives. This explains why our desire is never static even if it tends to crystallize around a highly specific constellation of longing. In the same way that human life consists of an open-ended process of becoming, our desire keeps adjusting itself in response to new objects and new kinds of stimuli; like everything else about human life, it amends its itinerary over time. If it did not, we would not be able to learn from our mistakes. We would be forever doomed to repeat the worst of our personal history. The repetition compulsion can easily give us the impression that this is the case—that we are fated to repeat our intersubjective misery until the day we die. Yet it would be far too convenient to leave things at that, for doing so would allow us to abdicate our responsibility for our romantic destinies.

But how can we be responsible for something that we cannot understand? How can we intervene in a part of our constitution that by definition resists our attempts to be the rational agents of our lives? These concerns reach the very core of contemporary ethics, namely, the question of how to reconcile the intrinsic opacity of human interiority with interpersonal accountability. They touch the larger problem of figuring out how we can admit that we do not have transparent access to our own motivations yet still acknowledge that we are profoundly and unquestionably responsible for how we treat others. That is, how can we conceive of ethics when the very status of the human being is uncertain—when the Freudian unconscious implies that none of us are the masters of our own house? I would like to devote the concluding pages of this book to this question because I think that it has far-reaching consequences for intimate relationships. I believe that there is perhaps nothing that impacts our love lives more than how we approach the tight knot of unconscious desire, human opacity, and ethical responsibility.

The Ethics of Relationality

Judith Butler expresses the dilemma perfectly when she states that there is an "unfreedom at the heart of love." By this she is referring not only to the idea that our patterns of love have unconscious motivations—and particularly that we are unconsciously driven to seek reparation for past injuries—but also to the idea that we owe our very being to the other. As I have explained, human subjectivity is inherently intersubjective in that we have a sense of self only to the extent that there are other people in the world who have contributed to our coming-into-being. We only have psychological depth and emotional capacity because we have a personal history of relationality—because others have over the years interacted with us in ways that have allowed us to craft a specific kind of inner life and, therefore, a specific kind of personality. Butler's point about this— one that I have also called attention to in this book—is that much of this self-crafting took place so early in our prehistory that we cannot approach it through conscious recollection. We have no choice but to resign ourselves to a radical "unknowingness" about key aspects of our own formation. This, in turn, complicates the issue of ethical accountability, for how can we give an account of our actions when we cannot fully account even for our own being?

Butler's solution to the dilemma is to argue that our opacity to ourselves represents an ethical opening in the sense that it makes us more tolerant of the opacities of others. The fact that we can never give a satisfactory account of ourselves renders us forgiving about the inability of others to generate seamless self-narratives. Butler therefore advocates an ethics of generosity that is based "on our shared, invariable, and partial blindness about ourselves." Our recognition that we routinely deviate from the story we tell about ourselves allows us to relinquish the mandate that others "be self-same at every moment." As Butler sums up the matter, "Suspending the demand for self-identity or for complete coherence seems to me to counter a certain ethical violence, which demands that we manifest and maintain self-identity at all times and require that others do the same." More specifically, our willingness to accept the inconsistency of both ourselves and others gives rise to an attitude of interpersonal humility that seeks to sustain a dialogue even when there seems to be no common ground—even when we cannot even begin to understand where the other is coming from. Because we know that the other may not entirely comprehend his or her own impulses, we persist in our attempts to communicate even in the absence of clarity.

There is maybe no better recipe for romantic success than this. As I have maintained throughout my discussion, a high degree of tolerance for interpersonal ambiguity is indispensable for the establishment and maintenance of intimacy. I have in fact tried to illustrate that the better we cope with relational uncertainty, the higher our chances for developing alliances that are strong enough to survive periods of confusion and commotion. When we forgo our demand for clarity, we also forgo our demand for stability, with the result that we may be able to interpret the inevitable upheavals of love as an intrinsic part of its unfolding rather than as a sign of its imminent undoing. In addition, it is true that our awareness of our own "unknowingness" can make us more forgiving of the "unknowingness" of others. However, it is possible to overstate the issue, as Butler perhaps does when she asserts: "I will need to be forgiven for what I cannot have fully known, and I will be under a similar obligation to offer forgiveness to others, who are also constituted in partial opacity to themselves."

Butler is here reasoning from a post-Levinasian perspective that is immensely popular in present-day ethical discourses, namely, the notion that because I am indebted to the other for my very existence, I am always already responsible for the other regardless of how he or she acts. That is, because I cannot have a self without the other, my ethical relationship to the other—and thus my willingness to forgive him or her for any and all infractions—is so foundational to my being that I cannot betray it without betraying myself. In Levinas's own words, "the fellow human being's existential adventure matters to the *I* more than its own, posing from the start the *I* as responsible for the being of the other." As to whether there is a limit to this responsibility is difficult to determine, for Levinas at times appears to propose that we are responsible even for those who persecute us. What most interests me in the present context, however, is the explicit connection that Butler draws between opacity and forgiveness. She seems to be saying that we, as well as others, deserve forgiveness for those things that we cannot understand about ourselves—that remain enigmatic, obscure, nebulous, or unintelligible about human interiority.

I would have to disagree. I think that positing inner opacity as semiautomatic grounds for forgiveness makes it far too easy for us, as well as for others, to relinquish responsibility at those very moments when self-interrogation would be most necessary. As much as I have advocated patience with the repetition compulsions of our loved ones, and as much as I have insisted that relationships possess the kind of emotional density that is often difficult to decipher, I think that there are times when the stance of "I did not know what I was doing" (or "my unconscious made me do it") becomes an all-too-expedient excuse for the most vicious interpersonal violence conceivable. I do not consequently believe that relational ethics is (or should be) a matter of uncritical forbearance for the unconscious fixations, passions, and obsessions of either ourselves or others. Quite the contrary, as I argued in chapter 2, it is a matter of claiming unconditional responsibility for our behavior even, and perhaps *particularly*, when it is unconsciously motivated. And it is a matter of expecting similar accountability from others, even when we might simultaneously empathize with their ongoing struggle to assume the considerable burden of that accountability.

We of course know that there will be lapses and moments of miscalculation; we know that we cannot expect perfection either from ourselves or from those we love. As I hope to have made clear, one of the main reasons we cannot control the outcome of our relationships is that we cannot always read, let alone regulate, the sentiments of either ourselves or others. What is more, we can neither guarantee nor demand a consistency of affection. Yet it is simply not the case that we—or those close to us—are merely the powerless pawns of opaque unconscious forces. To put the matter bluntly, having an unconscious does not annul our capacity for conscious reflection. And it certainly does not neutralize what is colloquially called bad conscience—the fact that we usually know full well the distinction between right and wrong, however unstable or open to change that distinction might be.

A Call for Accountability

As I argued in the last chapter, we routinely make life-shaping decisions without having all the facts. And we often act without being able to predict the consequences of our actions. But this does not absolve us of responsibility for our choices. Nor does it mean that we should automatically be forgiven for our missteps. For instance, if I am a medical student who harms a patient because I cannot yet tell the difference between one drug and another, I may garner some sympathy from those who understand my predicament. But I will still be held accountable. Why, then, should things be any different with unconscious motivations? If I consistently devastate my lovers because I am haunted by an unconscious desire to revenge the harm done to me in the past, am I somehow less to blame for their pain? Of course not! If those I hurt know about my wounding past, they may have some compassion for me. They may act leniently toward me, sometimes giving me a second, a third, or even a fifteenth chance. But this does not in any way exonerate me. And the further I stretch the kindness of others, the less excusable my behavior becomes. One lapse might be defensible. But when I am pushing against lapse number 15, it is time for me to take a close look at how my unconscious is running my life.

One of the main objectives of this book has been to show that we can work at developing a discerning relationship with our unconscious patterns so that we, over time, become better at defusing them before they get the better of us. This is not to say that we can (or should) control our unconscious desire, for this is obviously impossible. I simply wish to point out that having a desire is not the same thing as letting that desire run amuck in ways that hurt those we are supposed to love. In the same way that I do not opt to sleep with every person I am attracted to, I do not need to act on every impulse that arises from the muddy waters of my unconscious. The interval between impulse and action is where human consciousness has the power to intervene. The fact that there is an "unfreedom" at the core of our lives does not, therefore, mean that we have no freedom at all. It merely means that this freedom is never unconditional—and that sometimes we need to work quite hard to attain it. It means that we must make a sustained effort to avoid letting our habitual patterns of relating determine our behavior. This is why unconscious desire is not a province of inner opacity that escapes ethical accountability, but rather one of its centerpieces.

Major thinkers of the second half of the twentieth century (such as Adorno, Lacan, Foucault, and Derrida) had excellent reasons for deconstructing conventional Western notions of human will and agency. For one thing, they understood that the will to mastery had led to unimaginable atrocities, such as Auschwitz, Hiroshima, and colonial exploitation. And they also understood that the worship of agency had served a whole tradition of arrogance that had blinded humankind to its constitutive weaknesses. I have no quarrel with the major thrust of these critiques. But it seems to me that, somewhere along the line, we have turned a corner so that the renunciation of will and agency has begun to inflict its own particular brand of violence—one where people claim the right to do whatever they please on the pretext that they cannot help themselves (or that they cannot fully understand their own motivations). A good example of this is the "homosexual panic" defense—one that courts have some-times taken quite seriously—whereby straight men seek to justify beating up gay men because the very presence of homosexuality supposedly arouses their unconscious conflicts regarding their own sexuality, sending them into such a "panic" that they feel driven to annihilate the source of their anxiety. In instances such as these, inner opacity serves as a rationalization for criminality.

As I see the matter, the recognition that human will and agency are always limited should not be taken to imply that we have no will and agency whatsoever. Likewise, the awareness that we are inhab-ited by unconscious forces that make us partially unintelligible to ourselves does not signify that we are not responsible for our rela-tional choices. As a result, if I have less and less patience with the notion of being infinitely forgiving (infinitely accepting, infinitely indulgent, infinitely generous), it is because, frankly, I think that we could benefit from raising the standards of interpersonal account-ability for everyone involved. I think we could benefit from being a little tougher with both ourselves and others.

Steering Clear of Masochism

Butler, following Levinas, claims that "I cannot disavow my relation to the other, regardless of what the other does, regardless of what I might will." Why not? While it may be difficult for me to disavow some of my relationships, particularly those that galvanize the bedrock of my desire, where is the ethical advantage of indulging those who wound me? I may owe an existential debt to those who have over the years facilitated my process of coming-into-being. But does this condemn me to an indiscriminate (and utterly uncritical) patience with each and every person I meet, irrespective of how badly they behave? I may have started my life in a state of interpersonal vulnerability that made it impossible for me to walk away from those who chose to harm me, but what keeps me from doing so now? Surely there is a distinction between the idea that we are inhabited by an ontological otherness that we cannot denounce—that we only have a self to the extent that we partake in structures of sociality—and the idea that we cannot sever our connection to *specific* others who injure us.

Butler maintains that "if we were to respond to injury by claiming that we had a 'right' not to be so treated, we would be treating the other's love as an entitlement rather than a gift." Yet there is an enormous difference between feeling entitled to someone's love on the one hand and insisting on being treated well on the other. As a matter of fact, the two attitudes have no inherent connection whatsoever. I can respect the other's love as a pure gift—one that I cannot translate into an entitlement without violating it—while at the same time claiming the right not to be unnecessarily wronged.

One reason that it is essential for me to hold onto this right is that being too ready to forgive can in certain circumstances perpetuate a cycle of violence indefinitely. For instance, if I am a battered woman, my willingness to forgive my husband for hurting me is unlikely to prevent him from doing so again. If anything, he may feel that I have granted him an implicit permission to continue the cruelty. When I forgive too easily, I imply that the treatment I have endured is acceptable so that there is no demand on the perpetrator to change his behavior. In a sense, I deprive him of agency by suggesting that he does not need to carry the responsibility for his activities. I treat him as a child who does not completely understand the ramifications of his actions rather than as an adult who possesses the mental apparatus to accurately identify these ramifications. This infantilization of the other is, in fact, one of the main weaknesses of Butler's approach, for she seems to presuppose that the human subject never outgrows its immature state of primordial helplessness. Undoubtedly, there are ways in which this is true (a point I will return to below). But it would be insincere to say that, as adults, we lack the tools to assess the ethical implications of our various undertakings. Indeed, a large part of the process of transitioning from childhood to adulthood is coming to wield such tools.

While I appreciate the idea of staying benevolent with the opaque inner lives of others, I think that there is a threshold where such benevolence turns into masochism—where the line between generosity and self-injury becomes dangerously thin. Crossing this line does nothing for our ability to give and receive love, for beyond it resides abuse (the very antithesis of love). As convoluted as our relationships may sometimes get, we do usually know when we have veered into this region. There is no point in putting down roots there, for its terrain is so barren that it will over time extinguish the spark that gives us life.

Crossing the line between generosity and self-injury also does absolutely nothing for our status as beings of ethical capacity. Instead, it places an unreasonable burden on those who have been victimized, implying that their desire to hold the perpetrator responsible for his or her behavior represents an ethical lapse of some kind. It asks the victimized not only to bear the brunt of their victimization, but also to adopt a completely unrealistic stance of compassion for their victimizers. It is of course possible to be merciful and critical at once—to forgive without condoning the other's actions—but an ethics that perceives forgiveness as a precondition of full humanity (as an existential *given*) rather than as a conscious *choice* made by the victimized places the latter in an impossible bind: either forgive or show yourself to be less than human by defaulting on your ethical responsibility to forgive the other. Either way, the perpetrator gets off the hook while the weight of doing the right thing is squarely placed on the shoulders of the injured party. What is this if not an incredibly sophisticated version of blaming the victim?

Forgiveness can be a powerful act—one that can alleviate the long-term effects of victimization by returning to those who have been wounded the dignity of having the capacity to forgive. But if forgiveness is a nonnegotiable requirement for ethical humanity, what have we done with agency? And, equally important, what have we done with anger? Are we not suddenly suggesting that anger is no longer among the legitimate feelings of humankind?

Personally, I think this would be a huge mistake, for anger is one of the surest ways to return self-respect to the victimized; the ability to feel justifiable anger is at least as—if not more—empowering as the ability to forgive. Indeed, such anger has arguably been among the main motivators of many of the most liberatory political movements of history, including the collective upheavals of the last century (the civil rights movement, postcolonial struggles, women's liberation, etc.). Where would we be if the agitators of these movements had opted for forgiveness rather than sublime anger? Although I agree with Butler (and Levinas) that seeking revenge for one's victimization is not effective because it merely feeds the rivulets of violence, it seems to me that there is an important distinction between revenge on the one hand and the kind of anger that insists on holding others responsible for their actions on the other. After all, it is entirely possible to ask for accountability—and even for restitution—without trying to humiliate the other. Why, then, are contemporary ethical paradigms so fond of unconditional forgiveness, and so completely (and the irony of this is blatant) *unforgiving* of anything that falls short of it, such as good old-fashioned anger?

The Other Side

I began this book with a line from David Gray's bittersweet ballad, "The Other Side." The basic message of this ballad is that we cannot undo what has been done. We cannot take back a moment that has passed. We can only meet our loved ones on "the other side" of our blunders. But this does not mean that we are not answerable for our actions. While there is no use in crying over spilt milk, there is nothing to prevent us from picking up the mop and cleaning up our mess. We cannot cancel out our mistakes, but we can definitely learn from them so as to make sure that we do not repeat them endlessly. This is why I believe that if we consistently slip in the same way—and particularly if we repeatedly hurt those we love—it is not forgiveness that we need. Rather, we need to start paying closer attention to the invisible puppeteer that is pulling our strings and making us dance a contorted dance that will never earn us a standing ovation. Stubborn repetitions, in other words, are our wake-up call to the necessity of accepting full responsibility for how our unconscious habits structure our relational world. This is in part what Freud meant when he said that the purpose of the talking cure was to make the unconscious conscious.

We can only begin to change our patterns of relating if we first understand something about their unconscious causes. And we can only develop this understanding if we are willing to take a critical look at our past. This is why—and here I return to a concern raised in chapter 8—I tend to be suspicious of the spiritual notion of living fully in the present. I admit that the notion of a "pure" present that is not contaminated by the past may sometimes be freeing. There are times when it liberates us from a futile faithfulness to a past that has nothing to offer. But if it leads to a denial of the inherently historical character of human life—if it causes us to pretend that the repetition compulsion has no influence over our destinies—it can intensify already problematic interpersonal patterns. It can make us callous to the ways in which our unconscious demons are often directly responsible not only for our own suffering, but also for the suffering of those who share our lives.

This callousness is, strangely enough, explicitly endorsed by many popular spiritual approaches, including the philosophy of "nonviolent communication" that I criticized in chapter 2. As we learned, the inventor of this philosophy, Marshall Rosenberg, tells us that we are not responsible for the feelings of others—that people get wounded only to the extent that they "allow" themselves to be affected by the actions and statements of others. I already conceded that this approach has good intentions. Yet it completely ignores the fact that our unconscious patterns—not to mention our conscious choices—can inflict tremendous pain on others. More specifically, it replaces the therapeutic notion of ongoing self-inquiry with the idea that we can learn a set of quasi-mechanical rules for "nonviolent communication" that will help us better relate to others. These rules tell us how to express ourselves so that, for instance, certain words and phrases are acceptable while others are not. We are, in short, being told that there is a magic formula for successful relating, and that we can learn this formula by rote, as it were, in the same way that we once learned the multiplication table.

The humorous side of this is that one can end up with absurdities along the lines of "you should never say should" (as one eager adherent of this philosophy once told me). The tragic side is that the approach (unwittingly yet effectively) feeds the false self, rewarding stilted, affected, and pretentious modes of communication and relationality in the name of nonviolence. Instead of acknowledging the situation-specific complexity and changeability of human relationships, it attempts to convince us that its magic formula offers us a way out of the aporias of affect. Even worse, because this formula can become a screen for our unconscious demons—because it allows us to pretend that these demons are irrelevant—it can serve as a means of generating ever more cunning (usually passive-aggressive) ways of hurting others. It can make us ethically complacent by implying that our adherence to it frees us of the need to interrogate our unconscious motivations, let alone the impact of our actions and statements. After all, if others get upset by what we do or say, this is not our problem (since we followed the formula) but theirs (since they obviously have not yet internalized it).

According to this philosophy, hurt feelings result from our inability to master the correct methodology. In this manner, Rosenberg subtly yet decisively shifts the burden of ethics to those who are on the receiving end of interpersonal brutality, situating responsibility with those who dare to have bad feelings despite the formulaic propriety of others. This is why, even though Rosenberg emphatically preaches nonviolence, his approach can become a pretext for immense violence. Its resistance to the crucial Freudian idea that the past remains a living and breathing component of the present—one that we cannot banish through either rational resolutions or spiritual interventions—can cause massive ethical failure. It is, in short, explicitly designed to squander the wisdom of the past rather than to profit from it.

This, among others things, is why I have made it a central theme of this book to illustrate that the more we struggle to deny our history, the more likely it is that we will keep repeating it, even when doing so causes pain not only to us but also to those we love. The more we strive to denounce, downplay, or discredit our unconscious demons, the more damage they will inflict on our relationships. In contrast, our awareness of past mistakes—and even the regret and sorrow that we may feel about them—can teach us to relate more wisely in the present (and the future). It might even allow us to gradually sort through what is most hurtful about the past so that we can, over time, acquire more productive ways of being human; it might allow us to reach "the other side" of our most dogged relational dilemmas.

Continuing to Care

My approach to relational ethics could thus be said to be the exact reverse of that of Rosenberg. While Rosenberg asserts that we are responsible for our feelings but not for the emotional impact of our actions and statements, I believe that we can learn to monitor our actions and statements—and therefore their impact on others—but not our feelings. If there is some truth to Butler's argument that we never fully overcome the vulnerabilities of our infantile state, it is in the recognition that our psyches remain open to the world in ways that make us agonizingly susceptible to the poisonous arrows flung from that world. In addition, because our emotions have an unconscious component that connects us to our past, we cannot keep ourselves from being hurt by our interpersonal interactions merely by telling ourselves that we should (let alone by learning a set of rules).

This is what many "spiritual" gurus—Rosenberg and Eckhart Tolle, arguably, among them—are doing their best to disavow. They appear to presuppose that people have (or should have) impenetrable defenses that, when correctly activated, protect them against suffering originating from their surroundings—that people, in other words, operate from a platform of immense ego strength rather than from one of relative woundability. This begs the question of who these philosophies are aimed at. Might there be a connection between their insistence that the world cannot get to us against our will and the fact that their supporters seem to assume that most of us are suffocating under the crushing weight of our egos?

Philosophies such as these often start from the premise that our egos are so massive that they stand in the way of enlightenment—that the only way to actualize our sacred calling is to defeat the ego. Yet I am not at all certain that an excess of ego is a problem for the vast majority of human beings. It may be a disease that plagues the most privileged among us. But there are plenty of individuals whose egos are too fragile to begin with. There are plenty of people—those trying to survive in war-ravaged conditions, those who have been forced into diasporic exile, those who live in abject poverty, those who suffer from racial, ethnic, religious, sexual, or gender discrimination, etc.— who have been forcibly robbed of their egos and who are consequently struggling to reestablish a sense of legitimate personhood. Telling them to rid themselves of their egos is akin to ignoring all the sociopolitical and economic circumstances that make it difficult for them to develop an ego in the first place. It is akin to saying that there is something amiss with their attempts to carve out a firm foothold in a world that is making their lives unsafe and sometimes even unbearable.

Undoubtedly there are people who profess to be able fend off hurtful external stimuli. Some are even quite convincing. However, in most cases one gets the impression either that the individual in question is feigning impassiveness—that, deep down, he cares as much as the rest of us—or that he only appears untouchable because he has assembled an impenetrable barrier against the world. This barrier, like the false self, excludes the good as effectively as the bad, thereby bankrupting life, and sometimes even giving rise to a personality that seems strangely robotic. Such robotic people are often the first to insist that we need to free ourselves from our pasts. Those with a more agile understanding of human experience, in contrast, know that the past—no matter how conflicted, no matter how full of sorrows, torments, mishaps, abuses, or moments of utter emotional weariness—will always be an element of the present. They know that to declare otherwise will not help us in any way. Yet they also understand that it may be possible to work though the past in such a way that when this past speaks in the present—as it invariably will—it does so in a manner that is conducive to our ability to form loving bonds with others.

Even when our past pulls us toward the murkiest depths of our being, we can learn to bring it to bear on the present in life-enhancing ways. Most important, we can come to recognize that our past does not need to be idyllic for us to be able to step into the midst of life; we can come to accept a less than perfect past as a part of our inner composition without feeling that it will forever thwart us. This, in turn, may make it easier for us to accept the imperfections of the passing moment. When it comes to romance, it may allow us to understand that love can be at once perfect and imperfect, thrilling and boring, buoyant and heavy-hearted, rewarding and disappointing—that there is no one way to love, no one way to relate, for the simple reason that relationships are never reducible to a clear classification.

Sometimes our loves succeed. Other times they fail. Yet other times they succeed because they fail. There are times when our most demanding alliance is also our most valuable one. But then there are other times when the romantic challenges we endure are merely a means of hiding the utter banality of our relationship—when we hold onto an affair solely because its trials endow it with an artificial sheen of nobility. In the end, what matters is how we respond to the set of opportunities and ordeals that a given relational dynamic grants us; what matters is how we negotiate the field of enchantments and disenchantments that a particular alliance generates. This process of negotiation is where relational growth occurs, for relationships only thrive to the degree that it is engaged. In a way, the rhythm of a relationship is nothing but the rhythm of this process. The beat of a relationship is nothing but the beat of the struggle to sustain its aliveness against the debilitating inertia of ceasing to care. When love summons us, it asks that we care. Our faithfulness to this summons means that we continue to care even when we know that not caring would be a whole lot easier.

Index

abandonment, 25, 74

accountability, 10, 36, 42, 143; abdication of, 43; as burden, 163; ethics of relationality and, 160; opacity of human interiority and, 159; unconscious desire and, 163–65. *See also* responsibility

Adorno, Theodor, 164

affairs, casual, 71, 144

agency, human, 10, 164–65; accountability and, 166, 168; women as desiring agents, 111

anger, 36, 73, 168

anxiety, 6, 50, 68, 93; enigma of others and, 80, 81; "homosexual panic," 165; self-fragmentation and, 55

Aristophanes, 14, 17, 18

attraction, inscrutability of, 23

authenticity, 68, 99–100

Badiou, Alain, 118, 151

Barthes, Roland, 24, 25, 145

Bataille, Georges, 144

beauty, ideal, 47

Beauvoir, Simone de, 13, 59

becoming, process of, 55–57, 60, 86, 159; idealized image of other and, 103; reinvention of identity and, 58; true self and, 64

betrayal, 25, 74

Bollas, Christopher, 60

Butler, Judith, 160–62, 165, 166–67, 168, 171–72

caress, 25, 51–55, 67

"chemistry," 23

childhood, experiences of, 28, 35, 80, 167

and malfunctions of, 156; idealizations and, 107; love as gamble
and, 9; repetition compulsion
and, 28, 30, 32; short-lived, 144;
sliver of eternity and, 60; sus-
ceptibility to suffering and, 143;
transience of, 150
Phillips, Adam, 137–38
philosophy, 96
Plato, 47–48, 51–52, 59, 119
psychology, popular, 10, 35–36, 42,
72, 73, 111

rationality, 96, 98
relationality, 59–60, 72; ethics of,
160–63; "nonviolent communication" and, 170; solitude and, 93
relationships, 44, 69, 165; abusive
or codependent, 39, 42, 124, 167;
attempts to control trajectory of,
142–43; complexity of, 33, 170;
enigma of others and, 85; fidelity
to love and, 152–53, 154; idealization of lover, 94, 103, 106, 107–8;
keeping desire alive in, 105; lin-
gering imprint of passion in, 74;
management of repetition compulsions in, 40; mission of love
and, 148–49; mystery and, 86,
93; negotiation in, 143, 174; power
in, 36; renunciation of love and,
115–16; repeating patterns in, 27,
30; solitude and, 92; transience of
romance and, 144–46; turbulence arising from unconscious
patterns, 37–39; unattainable or
unavailable lovers, 111–12; unpredictable outcome of, 142, 146
repetition (patterns), unconscious,
27–28, 45, 169; compulsion to
repeat, 28–30, 94, 149, 159, 162;

management of, 39–44; "nonviolent communication" and, 170;
psychological triggers of, 34–36;
tenacity of, 158–59; turbulence in
relationships and, 37–39; world
structured by, 31–34
responsibility, 37, 40, 43, 143; awareness of behavior patterns and, 41;
evasion of, 36, 42; interpersonal,
10; repetition compulsion and,
159–60; ruptures of love and, 151;
for unconscious relational habits,
169. *See also* accountability
romance: adventure and, 143;
disappointment in, 72; family romance, Freudian, 159; as gamble,
9; loss and, 126; overinvestment
in, 59; transience of, 144–46
Rosenberg, Marshall, 36, 41, 169–71,
172

sadness, 128–32, 135, 137
Santner, Eric, 68, 84
science, 16, 96, 131
self-actualization, 4–6, 17, 68;
enigma (unknowability) of others
and, 88; losses of love and, 11;
narcissistic, 18; outside of love, 13;
relationality as form of, 59; social
identities and, 48
self-awareness, 40, 57, 114
self-help literature, 8, 71–72
self-other interaction, 4–5, 162, 166;
beloved as mirror, 17–19, 20, 24,
25, 26; boundary with others, 50,
54; dissolution/disintegration of
self, 50, 51, 144; enigma (unknowability) of others, 79–81, 82, 84,
87–88; fantasy of wholeness and,
17; idealization of other, 98, 100,
103; interiority of other, 101;